the glow-up manifesto

the glow-up manifesto

7 Mystic Keys to Transform Your Thoughts into Gold and Manifest Your Next-Level Life

mystic rainn

Copyright © 2025 by Mystic Rainn

Published in the United States by Sovereign Quill Press • Atlanta, Georgia

sovereignquillpress.com

All rights reserved. No part of this book may be reproduced in any form or by any electronic or mechanical means, including information storage and retrieval systems, without written permission from the publisher, except for the use of brief quotations in a book review.

The author of this book does not dispense medical advice or prescribe the use of any technique as a form of treatment for physical, emotional, mental, or medical conditions without the advice of a physician, either directly or indirectly. The intent of the author is to offer information of a general nature to support your personal growth and well-being. If you choose to use any of the information in this book, you do so at your own discretion. The author and publisher assume no responsibility for your actions or outcomes.

Mystic Rainn and Mystic Maven are trademarks of Mystic Visions Entertainment, LLC. Used with permission.

Sovereign Quill Press is a trademark of Sovereign Quill Press, LLC.

First Edition

Mystic Rainn

The Glow-Up Manifesto: 7 Mystic Keys to Transform Your Thoughts into Gold and Manifest Your Next-Level Life

Library of Congress Control Number: 2025913782

ISBN: 979-8-9992779-0-9 (hardcover)

ISBN: 979-8-9992779-1-6 (paperback)

ISBN: 979-8-9992779-2-3 (Ebook)

For the Mystic Mavens

contents

Preface	ix
manifesto (n.):	1
A Reality Check	3
The Riddle Holding You Back	11

the seven mystic keys

The First Mystic Key *Establish Awareness*	27
The Second Mystic Key *Challenge Your Beliefs*	41
The Third Mystic Key *Reframe Your Thoughts*	53
The Fourth Mystic Key *Shift the Vibe*	63
The Fifth Mystic Key *Move Like It*	75
The Sixth Mystic Key *Hold Your Position*	87
The Seventh Mystic Key *The Manifesto*	99

the glow-up

Main Character Energy	113
Dream Bigger, Babe *Your Vision Board Needs an Upgrade*	127
Call In Your Soulmate *Heart Rehab for the Heartbroken*	139
Transform Your Money Mindset	153
Rewrite the Rules *Redefine Success on Your Own Terms*	167
The Coronation	181

Afterword	185
Mystic Rainn	187
Also by Mystic Rainn	189

preface

For the ones who always knew they were meant for more.

This is not your average self-help book. I did not write this to give you fluff, cute affirmations, or another list of watered-down life tips you could have found on social media. I wrote this because I needed to say something real that could wake up the part of you that has been dozing off in the backseat of your own life. I wrote this because I remember what it feels like to know you were made for something bigger and still find yourself stuck in smallness. This is for the version of you who looks around and says, "There has to be more than this." This is for the part of you that never stopped dreaming, even when life tried to silence it.

Welcome to the Glow-Up.

We hear "glow-up" and think of pretty selfies and gym routines. Perhaps a new wardrobe haul on YouTube? But this book is not about surface changes. We are in the business of alchemy and transmutation. This is about turning your thoughts—the raw material of your existence—into gold. Not metaphorical gold. I

Preface

mean the kind of golden life that reflects your next-level self—the one you daydream about but have not yet let yourself fully claim.

When I say "Glow-Up," I am talking about becoming the fully expressed, unapologetically iconic version of you—the version that creates instead of reacts, the version that chooses instead of waits, the version that does not shrink for anybody, the version that does not ask life to give them something and instead demands payment—because life will now happen on your terms, no apologies.

There is a very specific frustration that comes when you are smart, self-aware, and spiritual… but still stuck. You know all the things. You have read the books, taken the courses, done the journaling, pulled the tarot cards (and, in my case, written a book on it), and saged your whole damn house, but you are still in the same place. You are in a place in life where you doubt yourself because you are playing small and still waiting for someone or something to give you permission to go all in on your life.

That frustration? I have lived it, and I know what it feels like to be overqualified in wisdom but under-activated in results. So, I stopped looking for permission. I let go of waiting for the sign when I realized that not every feather on the ground meant an angel was talking to me. Sometimes birds just drop them. I stopped asking, "Am I allowed?" and started deciding, "I am doing it," even when I did not know what to do.

And that is when everything changed.

This book is the result of that shift, and I wish I had it when I was trying to bridge the gap between

Preface

knowing and becoming, between desiring and doing, and between thinking about the life I wanted… and then just deciding to live it.

This book is broken into 7 Mystic Keys, not steps, because this process is not always linear. These are thought reprogrammers. Each key unlocks a new level of clarity and self-command within you. You may see yourself reflected in ways that make you squirm a little but grow a lot. You will have to release what no longer serves you—and that might mean identities, stories, excuses, and sometimes even people. But what is on the other side is worth it, because your life is not stuck. Your thoughts are. And once you change those? Everything else has no choice but to follow—because the Universe likes alignment.

If you have ever been told you are too much, too intense, too opinionated, too ambitious, or too loud, this book is for you. If you have ever played small to keep the peace, dimmed your light to make others comfortable, or denied your greatness because you did not want to make other people jealous, this book is for you. If you have spent your whole life being the responsible one, the strong one, the one who always keeps it together but secretly wonders when your glow-up is coming, this book is for you. If you are used to hiding behind your intellect, perfectionism, or spirituality because being seen still feels too risky—and less-than-smart people resent your wisdom—this book is your call to step up. I do not care how long you have been sitting on the sidelines or what your past looks like. If you are holding this book, then it is your time. Not because I said so, but because you said so.

Preface

You already have everything you need. This is not about fixing you, because you were never broken. This is about calling out and removing the mental noise that has been distorting your power. You do not need to be perfect to change your life. You just need to decide. That is it. Decision-making is the most useful spiritual tool that there is, and when you make one, the Universe reorganizes around it. Why? Because the Universe likes alignment.

You were born to live in full color and to manifest a life that feels like freedom. We do not shrink over here, and we damn sure do not dim our light. We are luminous beings who take up space.

manifesto (n.):

"A WRITTEN statement publicly declaring the intentions, motives, or views of its issuer."

It is a bold declaration of truth and a sacred rebellion against self-imposed limitations. A manifesto is not a passive collection of ideas; it is a decree, a spell, a call to action for the soul, and a set of instructions for reality. It does not ask for permission. It does not seek approval. It demands the transformation of reality for those who command it.

a reality check

LET ME BE CLEAR: you are far more powerful than you know, and the level of magic that courses through your veins is more potent than you will ever have the ability to comprehend with the human mind. The human mind has been conditioned to accept a reality of limitation, strife, and resistance. It does this not because the mind is weak, but because that was the agreement that was made prior to our incarnations into these bodies and into this collectively agreed-upon reality.

But here is the thing... that conditioning? It's like one of those puzzles that look impossible to solve until you realize that the missing piece was in your hand the entire time. What most people fail to understand is that this condition of the mind and life is simply a riddle. It is not the final outcome. This riddle is not meant to define all your thoughts, nor is it intended to create a permanent life experience, nor is it meant to be the be-all and end-all.

There is no pop quiz at the end of this journey; it is just a steady reminder of who you truly are. The point of the riddle is to solve it—or to solve the mind. It wants to be solved and has always been waiting for you to get the point. The point of the riddle is to remember that the mind is simply a vessel that holds your consciousness. The point of the riddle is to remember that you are in control of your mind—and you always have been—because you are the guardian of your consciousness.

Once you remember the riddle, you must then understand that it has always been you who has been creating and influencing your life's creations and, therefore, your experiences, and that it is you who has gotten yourself to where you are today, even if you think you made some wrong turns along the way. And here's the real tea: even if you've made some wrong turns along the way, you're still in the driver's seat, holding the map and the mindset (that I'll help you transform) to get wherever you want to go.

In fact, your mind is so strong that along your journey, you have managed to successfully convince yourself that you do not have power in your own life and that you are at the mercy of whatever life throws at you. That you are stuck or stagnant without making forward movement toward your goals. That you will never have the ability to accomplish your dreams. That you have run out of options. That you lack creativity or talent. That you are not lovable and will never be loved for who you really are. That no one cares about you and will never see you for who you are. That, perhaps, you are not as smart as you think you should be. That maybe you should have prioritized completing your homework while in school, or that you should have finished school in the first place. That you should lose more weight and reduce the size of your gut and thighs. That you will never be healthy. That you should have a better job or make more money. That you should speak up and stand up for yourself more often. That you will never have the resources to move or travel. That you cannot do this or that, or cannot have this or that, or cannot be this or that—and blah, blah, blah.

Whew! That is a lot of noise, right? It's like your mind is hosting a 24/7 roast at your expense, and you are just sitting there letting it happen. You are not the punchline of your own life; you are the main event. It is always something with you. Sometimes, you are like a boxer who has stepped into a ring but then forgotten you had hands.

In fact, your mind is so strong that it has convinced you to spend all of your beautiful life force and all of your power—and use it against yourself. And because your mind has the strength to repeatedly convince you that it is right, instead of using its force to build yourself up, you have used your power and force to tear yourself apart.

As a result, you have spent your lifetime fighting with yourself and calling yourself your own worst enemy. Do you not think it's a little foolish to make an enemy out of yourself? Why would you want to make an enemy out of a force that strong? Instead, you should work to befriend that force—and by a natural consequence of befriending that force, you would then befriend yourself for the first time in a long time. Would it not be nice to finally be friends with yourself, to be at ease within yourself? Honestly, you are too brilliant, too magical, and too destined for greatness to keep playing this tired game.

This is a hard pill for many of you to swallow. Some people will even say to me, "Hey! You don't know my life or what I've been through. Why would I choose to create that kind of experience for myself?" And to that, my response is: you are right; I do not know your life personally, nor do I know what you have been through. But this is what I do know about you that you have yet to learn for yourself—something that you have repeatedly refused to see: you are stronger than you know.

And if you thought that was hard to read, then now is the time for me to give you some more hard news. Contrary to the popular belief system you have been carrying throughout your entire life, you are not your circumstances. You are not your mistakes. You are not your past regrets or your previous embarrassing moments. You are not the one time you mixed up your words and accidentally said the wrong thing. You are not that failed relationship. You are not the job you got fired from. You are not that poor investment you made or that failed business venture. You are not the fight that you got into with your parents, spouse, or children. You are not that friendship that fizzled out. You are not that missed opportunity. You are not the test you flunked. And you are definitely not your middle school haircut —let's just agree to never talk about that again!

You are not the sum of your parents' mistakes. You are not your past, and you still have the opportunity to decide who you will become in your future. You are consciousness and the force behind everything. You are the power behind what gives life to your thoughts that shape your reality, and you are the only one who holds the key to unlocking the doors of possibility that, up until this point, you have been too scared to open. That magic that courses through your veins—and the very power that you have used to convince yourself that your self-imposed limitations are true—is the same magic and power that will free you if you choose to use it in a way that is more productive.

Let that marinate for a minute.

It is you who has created your entire reality around you—all of the good and all of the bad. I did not say that you *meant* to create your reality, but you must accept that you *did* create your reality. Acceptance is the only way that you will be able to change your circumstances. You created your reality with your thoughts, current belief systems, and the expectations that you have set for your life—many of which have been negative and self-harming. Yes, life will throw you curveballs and pop out of a corner with the occasional jump scare to check if you are still paying attention (life really loves the extra drama, right?). But even with those outside forces, you are still your own force, and whether you choose to succumb to those situations or rise above them is entirely in your control. It has always been up to you.

I know it sounds like a tall order, but the moment you realize that you have been holding the pen to your life's story the entire time—that is the moment that changes everything.

Once you begin to understand and develop the awareness that your thoughts and current belief system are creating your reality, guess what? You can start to change them. And once you begin to change your thinking, your life will begin to change, too.

I will level with you. It is not always that easy to accept that you have this kind of power, because once you accept this power, suddenly, you must take accountability for all the things that happen in your life. It is not easy to take responsibility for the way your life looks right now. In fact, it can be downright terrifying because once you realize you have the power to change everything, there are no more excuses.

There is no going back to your previous way of living. There are no more pity parties. There is no more waiting for someone else to ride in on a white horse to come and save you. There is no more blaming circumstances, people, or fate. It is all up to you. And honestly? This should be the best news that you have heard all day. Why? Because it means the ball is in your court. It means freedom.

However, there is beauty in it all being on you now, because that means you have the power to turn everything around, rewrite your story, and regain control of your life. Imagine what a life that you are directing would look like for you now that you know you have the ability to wake up tomorrow and decide that you are no longer going to be held back by those old, limiting beliefs that have kept you small and hidden from the world.

What would life look like once you start operating from the belief that you are worthy and that you are capable? What would life look like if you started moving from the space where you are more than enough, just as you are? Imagine setting aside all of your fear and self-doubt, or those old narratives that no longer serve you and never did. What would happen if you just decided, at this moment right now, that you were going to think differently?

Imagine waking up with the energy of someone who knows they are unstoppable. You smile at your reflection because you can finally see the magic everyone else has always seen in you. You walk into a room not just to take up space but to own it.

What could you achieve if you believed in yourself fully and removed the boundaries to your success? If you used that magic within you and approached your life from a place of confidence, strength, and power? If you moved with the understanding that every thought you think is actively shaping and transforming the world around you? How would your life change if you simply used your power to think thoughts that built you up instead of tearing you down?

The answer is that your life will begin to change. Maybe not all at once, but gradually, subtly, a little bit here and there. And then, BAM! Suddenly. Next thing you know, the things you once convinced yourself were impossible would suddenly start to feel like they were within reach. The things that give you stress and anxiety will no longer keep you up at night. The things that you want would start showing up in your life, not because a shooting star answered your wish, but because you changed your thinking and aligned with your thoughts.

This is a universal law, and the law does not discriminate. What you think, you become. Period.

So, here is what you are going to do. You will take

control of your mind, stop letting your thoughts run you instead of you running them, stop making yourself your enemy, and instead make yourself the ultimate ally.

In this book, we will call out the thoughts and beliefs that are shaping your reality, and I will give you the tools to start shifting them in ways that will transform your life. You will learn how to recognize and release those mental and emotional blocks that have been holding you back and replace them with a belief system that builds you up.

It is time to stop living small and settling for less than you deserve. And baby, you deserve it all.

Ready to change your thinking and, with it, your life?

Let's get started.

the riddle holding you back

WE WILL GET to the part about changing your life in a second, but before you can even think about that journey, you first have to develop an understanding of the vehicle that is going to take you there—your mind. Even though it sounds simple, this process is not easy. How can you change your mind if you do not know how it actually works? To answer these questions, it is necessary that we look at what I like to call "the riddle of the mind."

When you think of the word "riddle," what comes up for you? Is it a challenge or a puzzle? Perhaps it is something that requires creative thinking to solve. This is exactly how I want you to begin seeing your mind, not as an enemy or this thing that is working against you. It is not inherently flawed or broken. Once solved, it is a puzzle that opens up a new reality and experience for you.

The mind is neutral and is not inherently positive or negative, neither good nor bad. It is simply a tool to be used and a computer that processes incoming information, stores your experiences, and helps you make sense of your world. The problem is that you have forgotten that you are the master of this tool, and only you have the password to unlock the computer. You have grown accustomed to letting your mind run the show and make the rules by allowing old beliefs and unexamined thoughts to dictate your life without realizing that you have the power to change the story at any time.

The riddle of the mind is that while it looks like it is in control, it has always been waiting for you to take the reins. The mind, like a computer, functions on default operating settings until you consciously step in and rewrite the program. It is like an outdated app on your phone. Until you update it, it will keep running the same old programs in the background, even if they no longer serve you.

One of the most important shifts you need to make in solving this riddle is understanding that your mind is a servant, not a master. Over time, you have become so identified with your thoughts that you believe they define you. You think that if you are experiencing a negative thought, such as "I am not good enough" or "I will never succeed," then that thought must be true for you. However, this is not the case, as it is merely a thought.

Thoughts have no meaning until you assign them a meaning. Your thoughts are not facts. They are just thoughts. Just like you are not your mind, you are the awareness behind your mind. When you grasp this, everything changes. You realize that you do not have to accept every thought that crosses your mind. You can question it. You can challenge it. You can decide whether or not to believe it. This is where your true power lies, and this is how you solve the riddle.

The primary way your mind keeps you stuck in the riddle is through fear. It convinces you that stepping out of your comfort zone is dangerous because it equates comfort with safety, which is why it clings so tightly to things that are familiar. Even when the familiar is limiting or painful, your mind would rather stay in a job you hate or a relationship that does not serve you. Why? Because the unknown feels risky.

Fear is your mind's way of protecting you from perceived threats, but the problem is that it does not know the difference between real danger and imagined danger. It is only responding to the idea of danger. Your mind also responds to the thought of failure, rejection, or embarrassment the same way it would respond to any life-threatening situation because all of those things seem dangerous, and the mind is incapable of categorizing threat levels. It will then trigger your fight-or-flight response, flooding your body with stress hormones and urging you to retreat to safety. Your mind's definition of "safety" is based on what you have experienced in the past. If you have experienced failure, it will try to protect you from future failure by making you feel afraid to try again. Your mind is just doing its job by protecting you from pain, but in the process, it keeps you locked in a cycle of fear and limitation.

The next part of the riddle is that you often over-identify with your caveman's brain and "thinking mind," or the part of you that is always analyzing, problem-solving, and planning. Although it may be an asset, it can also become a trap if you rely on it too heavily. Most people become so focused on thinking their way through life that they lose touch with their intuition and inner knowing.

The caveman's brain thrives on control and certainty, and it wants to have all the answers to every question. It believes that it is capable of predicting the future and has the ability to solve every problem before it even happens. So much so that it will have you up until the early hours of the morning agonizing over a pretend problem that has not occurred and probably will never occur. Nonetheless, you are convinced that this is the time to solve it. And when you cannot arrive at an answer, you spend the next day filled with anxiety over an imaginary problem that you have created, and your mind has convinced you that the whole thing was real.

Because the mind does not like uncertainty, it tends to conjure up worst-case scenarios. It will say things like, "What if you fail?" or "What if people do not like you?" or "What if you are not good enough?" These thoughts are just another way the mind tries to protect you from danger by keeping you in the familiar. This is why there is a disconnect between what you want to do and what you are doing. Your desires and actions do not match because you are currently allowing your mind to drive instead of being in the driver's seat. It is not because you are not strong enough; it is because you were missing this critical piece of information: the mind is a riddle that wants to be solved, and you can control it if you wish.

All of your desires reside on the other side of what is comfortable and familiar. If you want to experience those desires, you must change your thinking around what is possible for you. Because this feels threatening, the mind will fight back, but you must not let it win. You must hold your position by committing to your desires until your old belief systems are silenced.

All thoughts are creative, making it important for you to become the conscious creator of your thoughts. Most people run on autopilot and have minds that habitually repeat old, limiting thoughts and beliefs. As a conscious creator, you must learn how to step in and take control of your mind by choosing thoughts that align with the life you actually want to create. This will help you reprogram your thinking and live a life that is more fulfilling.

This is important to grasp because the mind can be your best ally and number one supporter with conscious control. But if you let it roam free, it will convince you that it is the enemy. As a child, my mother would say, "An idle mind is the Devil's workshop," and she would make sure that I did not get the opportunity to fall too deep into the negative depths of my mind.

Part of the riddle is that the mind was not designed to help you grow and thrive; it was designed to help you survive. It is not occupied with your greatness because it is diligently working to keep you safe by fulfilling its primal duty. Its caveman-brain job is to keep you away from predators, and it does that by keeping you quiet, small, and hidden. By camouflaging you and blending you into society—because if you are not seen by a bear, then you cannot be mauled by a bear.

Let that marinate for a second.

Due to the mind's primary function, it does not prioritize pushing you to the top of what you consider success. It does not care about helping you achieve your biggest dreams or guiding you on your path to spiritual enlightenment. The mind's autopilot default setting is keeping you alive. It does this by repeating what it already knows how to do, and this is how you get trapped in the familiar. It will do this even if the familiar is a painful experience, because the mind already knows how the situation will play out. And because it is predictable, the mind will keep you there, because it feels safe.

New things are not predictable. To the caveman's brain, anything new means that there is a bear on the other side. This is why you can have the sincerest desire to change, grow, and expand, but still battle with resistance. This is what causes the push and pull inside of you: the desire to change, but the feeling of being stuck where you are.

This is also how people end up in cycles of self-sabotage. It is the same reason we stay in jobs that we hate with a boss who should never be in a leadership position. It is why we end up in abusive relationships, whether that is physical, mental, or emotional. And it is why we can sometimes find it difficult to remove ourselves from situations that drain us of our energy, love, and joy. We have developed habits of playing small, shrinking ourselves, and dimming our light, because somewhere deep inside, our minds believe that staying in our current situation, no matter how unsatisfying, is safer than that make-believe bear on the other side of what is new.

the conscious mind: the caveman's brain

To understand this riddle more deeply, let us examine the key players shaping our thought and belief patterns, which influence how we view and interact with our world.

The mind is layered, and starting at the "top" sits the conscious mind, which is the part of our awareness that we actively engage with. It is the voice inside your head that is trying to help you navigate through daily life. It is the part of your mind that evaluates information and makes decisions. Anytime you decide what to eat for dinner or how to solve a problem at work, you are engaged with your conscious mind.

Your conscious mind is like a ship. You are the captain of the ship. If you do not actively steer the ship or give commands to the crew, the ship and everyone on it will veer off course. Even though the conscious mind is tasked with decision-making, it only makes up a portion of the mind as a whole due to its limitations. The conscious mind can sometimes become stuck as it over-relies on its need for logic and reason.

It is occupied with having immediate experiences and can only work in the present moment by focusing on whatever is directly in front of you. The results of this can be temporary and fleeting because it creates challenges when trying to change. Think about a time when you tried to incorporate something new into your lifestyle. Perhaps you wanted to change your eating habits or start going to the gym more regularly. You did it for a couple of days or even a few weeks, but eventually, you fell back into your old patterns. Your conscious mind is incapable of making the change by itself, which is why it is the caveman's brain.

If you want to expand your consciousness, move beyond the caveman's brain, and solidify your changes, you must learn how to balance the conscious mind with the next mind levels.

the subconscious mind: the servant

The subconscious mind sits in the "middle," and its job is to be a servant to the conscious mind. This is why, as captain of the conscious mind, you must be intentional about the commands you give, because whatever you think or say will be followed by the subconscious mind without question or judgment. Your thoughts are your commands, and your servant-subconscious mind will work to carry out its instructions. This makes it like a dusty storage closet that holds every repeated thought, emotion, and belief.

It will act as a repository for your old belief systems until you change your thinking by cleaning out the old thought patterns. It cannot distinguish between beliefs that are helpful and those that are harmful. It can only carry out the instructions that it receives. It does not decide what to do based on whether a thought is positive and empowering or if it is negative and self-sabotaging; it just does what it is told to do. It never stops working to serve you, and for twenty-four hours a day, it will work to carry out anything you feed to it.

The subconscious mind does not evaluate information in the same way as the conscious mind. It does not question any command that is given and will simply follow it without hesitation. This is what makes it a servant. The problem is that the current commands it is following are old, and many commands that were given to it you were not aware of, or they were given to it in your childhood. Most of them are outdated, limiting beliefs that were picked up from your parents, teachers, friends, or society, and over time, they have rooted themselves in your subconscious mind. For example, if you constantly heard as a child that "money does not grow on trees," this belief may have settled into your subconscious mind, making it difficult to experience financial abundance even though now you are an adult. You may carry a belief that money requires hard work, so your conscious mind commands your subconscious mind to work hard, leaving you feeling tired and burned out. Perhaps you have a belief that you must save more than you spend, which commands your subconscious mind to hold onto money, making it difficult for you to spend money on things or experiences that would bring you joy.

This is why you must give your servant-subconscious mind new commands to replace the old instructions that it was given a long time ago. The goal here is to transform it into a servant that works for you, not for those outdated beliefs. You are the captain, and it is your ship.

the unconscious mind: the roots

The unconscious mind sits on the "bottom" and is the garden for the roots from which all things in your mind and belief system grow. If your roots are not healthy, then how you use your mind is not healthy. A lot of this work will require that you tend to the roots in your garden to make them healthy again, so that what grows from them are positive things that create fulfillment in your life. When the unconscious mind is forgotten about, or the garden is left unattended, it can turn into a graveyard where everything you have buried resides. It is the deepest level of your mind and contains your forgotten memories. It is where your primal drive and instincts live and is the home of your deepest desires and fears, which influence your conscious mind on the "top."

Because it acts like a graveyard when left unattended, all things that reside here are pushed deep down and out of your immediate awareness. Painful emotions, unresolved conflicts, and traumas can grow roots here and create patterns that play out in your life without you knowing where it is coming from. It can also shape your personality, your perceived personal identity, and your feelings about your life path and whether you are capable of fulfilling that path. When you find yourself stuck in a cycle of self-sabotage—perhaps you keep picking the wrong relationships or pushing away success—the root of the reason for why you are doing that is in the unconscious mind.

The three minds are always communicating with each other, and it is important to understand how they work together because then you will have the ability to work with them instead of feeling like they are always working *you*. While the conscious mind can make decisions that the subconscious mind will follow, the unconscious mind holds the reasons why the conscious mind has chosen a particular decision. The unconscious mind will trick you into believing that it has the final say and that you are powerless against your thoughts, but you have the ability to override the patterns in the unconscious mind by using your conscious mind to make different choices.

Let's say you've made a decision to pursue a new relationship or start a new job; if the roots in your unconscious mind are holding on to the fear of failure or rejection, it may trick you into believing that you can't do it. Those fears may have been triggered by a childhood event that left you feeling inadequate and are now influencing your behavior without your awareness. Your conscious mind will start to sabotage your efforts by making decisions that steer you away from those outcomes because it believes that it is protecting you. The unconscious mind tricked it into thinking it had perceived a threat. These decisions may influence you to procrastinate on sending your resume or lead you to choose a partner who reinforces old, unhealthy dynamics.

When your conscious, subconscious, and unconscious minds are working together in harmony, you become unstoppable because you are now intentionally directing your life. To change your thinking and ultimately change your life, you must work with your conscious mind to set new goals and intentions that your subconscious mind can follow, and work on the roots of your unconscious mind by tending to the things that you have left buried and unresolved.

Here's how you can begin that process:

1. **Start by paying attention to your thoughts.** What do you tell yourself on a daily basis? What are the stories you repeat to yourself about what you can achieve? Are these thoughts limiting?
2. **Ask yourself, "How do these thoughts serve me?"** "Is this really true?" Was it initially put in place to protect you? Was it something that your parents said to you as a child? Does it still serve you today?
3. **Reframe your thoughts with something that benefits you by turning a limiting thought into a possibility.** A very simple example of this is turning "I cannot do it" into "I can do it." Even if you do not believe it yet, you have opened yourself up to the possibility.

The journey of changing your thinking is not about erasing your past or healing all of your traumas overnight. It is about working with all parts of your mind to bring them into alignment. It just so happens that bringing them into alignment will create a healing effect, helping you see that you are in control of your reality and not a victim of circumstance.

The Riddle: What pretends to lead the way, but only follows orders and speaks with your voice, but is not you?

Answer: Your mind.

the seven mystic keys

the first mystic key
Establish Awareness

YOU HAVE SPENT your life curating a web of lies that have wound you up so tightly that you could not escape from Charlotte's web if you wanted to. At least, not by yourself. If you were successful at doing it by yourself, you would have done it already.

Changing your thought patterns and belief systems to spark that ultimate mark of expansion, the glow-up, requires that you bring to the forefront all of the fiction that you have manufactured throughout your lifetime. Of course, not all of the lies manage to work themselves in there consciously, but nevertheless, they still exist. Even if you did not intend to adopt a certain belief system, the burden of responsibility is on you to hold. You are the only one who can reach into the depths of you to pull out the beliefs that no longer work for you. It is up to you to identify them and bring them into your full awareness. You must commit to seeing things exactly as they are in order to change them into what they will be.

You are telling yourself stories that keep you exactly

where you are, gaslighting yourself into believing that the reason you are stuck is because of something external. It is the economy. It is the way you were raised. It is your zodiac sign, your past life karma, your childhood trauma. Oh, I know the drill, and I've heard it all. I have even said some of it myself. And while yes, these factors may have shaped the foundation of your thought patterns, they are not the reason you are still here, repeating the same cycles, banging your head against the same damn wall. You are the reason.

You are in this position because you refuse to see things exactly as they are. You are still telling yourself comforting little fairy tales about why you cannot move forward, about why your hands are tied. And let me tell you, babe, you have woven together a masterpiece of fiction. If there were Oscars for self-deception, you would be up on that stage giving your acceptance speech right now.

And I can already hear you now, "But Mystic Rainn, I do not believe in lies! I believe in science! I believe in facts!" That is cute. Let me give you an example of how deeply entrenched your beliefs are without you even realizing it.

Remember that time you woke up one morning and looked in the mirror? Your first thought was, "Ugh, I look terrible today." You did not question it. You just accepted that thought as a fact, as if the Universe had sent you a certified letter overnight confirming that you were indeed hideous that day.

Then you went out into the world, and someone complimented you, "Oh, you look great today!" Did you accept it? No. You laughed it off, saying, "Oh, I just threw this on." Because in your mind, the first thought, which was the lie you told yourself, was the truth. And anything contradicting that you already deemed as wrong.

See how this works? You create a belief, and then you reinforce it by rejecting anything that does not fit inside of it. You have been living inside a mental echo chamber that only allows in the thoughts that validate your worldview, and anything outside of it gets tossed out like an expired carton of milk.

And listen, I am not even mad at you for it. Your mind is just doing what it has been programmed to do, which is to protect you. The problem is that your mind is unreliable. It is out here crafting elaborate storylines with plot twists and emotional drama just to keep you exactly where you are.

Your mind is like that one gossipy friend who is always spreading (mis)information about other people and things, but says it with so much conviction that you almost believe them.

You know the friend I am talking about. The one who swore up and down that chewing gum takes seven years to digest. That is your mind. Your mind is that friend. And unfortunately, you have been believing everything it tells you.

If you want to change your life, you have to start questioning the stories you tell yourself. You have to commit to seeing things exactly as they are, not as you wish they were, not as you fear they are, but as they actually exist.

Okay, so you believe you're just "bad with money." You have been telling yourself this for years. "Every time I try to save, the check engine light comes on." And because you have taken this belief and made it your gospel, you never even question it. You never stop to ask yourself if it is true. You never examine where it came from. You just accept it and keep reinforcing it every time you make a purchase you regret. Every time you see your bank account dwindle.

What is actually happening is that you just never learned how to manage money. But instead of acknowledging that, you have codified it into your identity. And because you believe it so deeply, your actions always reinforce it. You do not read books on finance. You do not seek out resources. You do not challenge yourself to grow in that area.

Do you see how insidious this is? The moment you believe something, you stop questioning it. And the moment you stop questioning it, you cement it into reality.

This applies to every aspect of your life. Your beliefs about relationships, success, happiness, worthiness, and everything else you believe are shaping your reality. And if you're getting triggered right now, then that's good. That means we are getting somewhere.

Yes, the world is unfair. Yes, you have been dealt hardships. But those are not reasons to stay stuck. They are not excuses to stop growing. They are the exact reasons you must wake up and shake yourself loose from the stories you have been telling yourself. It is time to see yourself clearly.

The way forward is through intentional self-inquiry and brutal honesty with yourself. The next time you feel resistance, stop and ask yourself, "Where is this coming from?" "Whose voice is this?" "Is this belief actually mine, or did I get it from somewhere or someone else?" You must become the detective of your own mind, hunting down limiting beliefs like they owe you money. Because, in reality, they do. They have stolen your potential, your confidence, and your future. And the only way to reclaim what is rightfully yours is to identify and dismantle them one by one. However, before you can dismantle it, you must first identify it.

Most people walk around with beliefs they never chose. They were handed these beliefs like hand-me-down clothes from an older sibling, clothes that did not fit, were not their style, and frankly smelled a little *off*. And yet, they wear them anyway because it never occurred to them that, as adults, they now have a choice. This choice includes deciding to continue to wear the clothes or making an empowered decision to take them off.

Awareness is the moment you look down and realize, "Wait a minute, this over-starched dress is two sizes too small and belongs to my great-aunt Rolie—why am I still wearing it?" It is the realization that some of the things you have been living by and defining yourself through were not actually yours. They were given to you, and you never questioned whether you wanted to keep them. But before you can question them (and oh, we will get to that in the next chapter), you have to see them first. And that is where developing awareness comes in.

The first step is to recognize the moments when your autopilot kicks in. Do you know the feeling when you are coasting through your day, responding to life in a way that feels a bit automatic, like a computer program running in the background of your mind? Someone gives you a compliment, and instead of accepting it, you deflect. That is a script. You see someone else succeeding, and a voice in your head says, "That could never be me." That is a script. You get excited about an idea, and before you even take the first step, another voice shuts it down with, "Who do you think you are?" Again, a script.

Your job, for now, is not to fight these thoughts. At least, not yet. Right now, you are just going to notice them. To catch them in the act, like a sneaky raccoon digging through your trash at midnight. There is no need to chase it away with a broom just yet, shouting at it. Just watch. See what it is up to and notice its patterns.

A great way to do this is through observation without judgment. Most people judge themselves harshly when they catch a negative or limiting thought. They think things like, "Ugh, why do I always think like this?" Or "I need to stop being so negative." But that is like yelling at a raccoon for being a raccoon. It cannot help that it always ends up in the trash; it just does. Judging does not change anything. It just increases the level of frustration you already feel with yourself. It is counterproductive.

Instead, think of yourself as a scientist running an experiment. Your only job is to collect the data. Every time a limiting thought arises, simply acknowledge it and mentally take note of it the way a scientist would. *Interesting. This thought showed up when I was about to try something new.* No judgment, no reaction. Just an observation.

Another helpful way to develop awareness is by listening to your body. Your mind might be slick, but your body never lies. Pay attention to when you tense up or when your stomach starts doing somersaults. Are your shoulders creeping up to your ears? These are signs that something deeper is happening beneath the surface.

Maybe you are about to speak up in a work meeting, and suddenly, your throat tightens. Or maybe you are about to charge more for your services, and you start feeling like you want to vomit. These physical reactions serve as clues or breadcrumbs, leading you straight to the limited beliefs that have been shaping your reality.

Then, go even deeper by paying attention to your emotional reactions. The things that trigger you hold valuable information. If a certain type of person annoys you, or if you get defensive when certain topics come up, there is likely a belief lurking beneath the surface.

Maybe seeing someone own their confidence irritates you because, deep down, you were taught that confidence is arrogance. Maybe watching someone take up space makes you uncomfortable because you were taught to be small and accommodating.

These triggers are not random. They are like little flashing neon signs pointing directly to the beliefs that have been running your life without your permission. And once you start noticing them, you can no longer pretend they do not exist. You will start to see them everywhere.

Speak your thoughts out loud. There is something about hearing your own words that makes them real in a way that just thinking about them does not. If you catch yourself thinking, "I could never do that," say it out loud and listen. Really listen. Does it sound true? Does it sound like you? Or does it sound like something you absorbed from the world around you?

Sometimes, the sheer act of hearing your thoughts outside of your head is enough to make you go, *wait a damn minute. Do I actually believe that?* But again, we are not questioning them yet. For now, we are just gathering evidence and building awareness.

be in the *now*

Awareness begins right here, right now, in the present moment. You cannot see reality if your mind is trapped in the past or lost in the future. The moment is not over yonder somewhere. The moment is here.

To ground yourself in the present:

1. Breathe! Your breath is probably shallow right now. Take five deep breaths and focus entirely on the sensation of air entering and leaving your body.
2. After taking a breath, start to engage your senses. What do you see, hear, smell, taste, and feel right now?
3. Set a timer for two minutes and simply

observe your current surroundings. Do not label or judge. Just notice.

remove the meaning

One of the biggest blocks to awareness is imposing meaning on what you see instead of simply witnessing it. When you impose meaning, you do so through the lens of your limited beliefs. It is not objective, and it is not neutral. You cannot dismantle your beliefs if you are busy judging what you see.

Try this:

1. Pick an object in front of you. A cup, a plant, your hand. It can be anything.
2. Look at the object without attaching a story. Instead of saying, "This is my favorite glass that I bought that one time I was drunk at Mardi Gras," simply observe that *it is round, clear, and smooth.*
3. Practice this kind of seeing with people, experiences, and even emotions. Recognize them without judgment.

expand your perception

Awareness requires that you see what is present and what is real, not just what you want or expect to see. Believe it or not, many of you want to see limitations because, at this point, limitation is your comfort zone.

How do you expand your perception?

1. Make it a goal each day to notice five things you have never noticed before in a familiar space.
2. Walk into a room and scan the space slowly. What details do you usually overlook?
3. Sit in a public place and simply observe people without forming opinions about them.

practice stillness

Stillness sharpens awareness by removing distractions. Reality will distract you with its noise and convince you that the chaos holds merit when it really is just a distraction. You can drown out the noise by slowing down reality and making it "still."

To practice:

1. Find a quiet space and sit with your eyes open.
2. Focus on a single point in the room.
3. Allow your thoughts to rise without engaging them. "The fries I ate today were soggy." "What is that weird spot on the wall?" "Is today trash day?" Just watch them come and go.
4. Do this for five minutes each day.

be the observer

The observer has the ability to see reality without reacting to it emotionally. View your thoughts as if you were an independent third party that is taking its first field trip around your limited mind. Pretend that you do not have any clues or context for why you are experiencing what you are experiencing; you only have the understanding that you are experiencing it.

To be the observer:

1. Throughout your day, take mental notes: *I am noticing frustration. I am noticing tension in my body.*
2. Instead of saying, "I am angry," say, "I am experiencing anger."
3. Make a shift from being your emotions to witnessing them.

daily reflection

Reflection is what elevates this practice from an activity and solidifies it into a skill. To cement your newfound observations into your awareness, try this end-of-day awareness practice:

1. Before bed, sit with your journal and ask, "What did I see today that I had never noticed before?" "Did I make any assumptions?" "Were they accurate?" "How did my awareness change throughout the day?"
2. Write your reflections without judgment. Just observe.

choose clarity

Take a deep breath, close your eyes, and say these words internally: *I choose to see the world exactly as it is. Because I said so.* Now, open your eyes and look around.

The world is no different than it was before, but now *you* are. You have acquired the first Mystic Key and are now seeing the truth with clarity.

You are aware.

---

glow-up activation: truth or dare

Ask yourself the following disruptive questions, one by one. After each question, sit quietly and answer honestly. Do not filter your answers or try to be "nice." Be as raw and unapologetic as possible.

1. *What belief or story do I hold that keeps me from reaching my fullest potential?*
2. *What am I most afraid of—really, truly afraid of— that I have not been able to admit?*
3. *What is the most uncomfortable truth about myself that I have been avoiding?*
4. *Where in my life am I accepting mediocrity because I am too scared of success or failure?*
5. *If I had to stand up and speak my truth right now, what would it be?*

For each answer you gave, identify the fear or limiting

belief it represents. Then, dare yourself to challenge that fear directly. This is not about positive affirmations; this is about doing something that feels downright uncomfortable and breaks the hold of the old pattern.

the second mystic key
Challenge Your Beliefs

PART OF GLOWING up is having the ability to reclaim your sovereignty. It is bigger than just changing how you think. It is about understanding that changing how you think simultaneously dismantles everything you have been taught to think. As you strip away the layers of your indoctrination, you are left with your raw self—the version of you that you were always meant to be. Your next-level self.

This uncovering leads to the rediscovery of your personal power and the inherent freedom that you possess as a sovereign, divine being. As a sovereign, you must exercise discernment, even when it pertains to yourself. Are your current thoughts and beliefs built to serve you to the highest level? If your immediate answer is no, then it is time for us to rip it apart.

You see, most people walk around carrying thoughts they did not even choose. Thoughts planted in them by their parents, teachers, a childhood best friend who once told them they would never make the varsity team, or that one ex who had the audacity to say they were too much. They took in thoughts as truth and never once stopped to ask, "Is this even mine? Or is this some secondhand trash I have been lugging around like a family heirloom I did not ask for?"

Take, for example, the person who grows up hearing, "It is hard to make money." They internalize it and absorb it into their bones. Before they know it, they are an adult who winces at every purchase over ten dollars, terrified that they will wake up and their bank account has just... vanished. Never mind that we live in a digital world where money, quite literally, is not even tangible most of the time. But that fear is real because they never thought to ask, "Is this true, or is this just some hand-me-down scarcity mindset from someone who struggled but was not strong enough to question why?"

Or let us talk about the person who was told as a child, "You are not creative," just because they did not draw inside the lines or because their second-grade teacher did not like their macaroni art. Fast-forward twenty years, and they are sitting at a desk, stuck in a job they hate, suppressing every dream of writing a book, painting, or launching that candle-making business they secretly fantasize about. Why? Because they never stopped to challenge the thought, "Maybe I was never bad at art. Maybe I just had a hater for a teacher."

Thoughts shape reality, and the dangerous thing is that they do so whether they are true or not. That is why you see people walking around with the wildest, most unhinged confidence while others who are far more talented, far more brilliant, are doubting themselves into irrelevance. The only difference? One person decided their thoughts were trash and tossed them out like expired milk, while the other kept drinking the sour stuff, wondering why their stomach hurt.

When was the last time you challenged your own thoughts? Think back to a time when you did not go for something because you "just knew" you were not good enough. That was a thought you should have thrown straight into the dumpster, but instead, you let it sit there like old leftovers. Perhaps you didn't apply for the job because you told yourself, "They would not pick me anyway." Perhaps you didn't message that person you were interested in because you assumed, "They are out of my league." Perhaps you didn't post that video or launch that business because a voice in your head said, "Who do you think you are?" And because you never questioned that voice, because you forgot who and what you are, you obeyed it.

Your thoughts are not facts. When you are at your worst, your thoughts at best are suggestions. Some are helpful, like "You should probably bring an umbrella today." Others are downright disrespectful, like, "No one wants to hear what you have to say." The problem comes when you accept every thought as a fact instead of what they really are, which are possibilities. Options. Not laws chiseled in stone.

Some of these thoughts are so outdated that they might as well be from a cassette tape found in your grandma's attic. Thoughts like, "You have to work yourself to the bone to be successful." Trash. "If you are not struggling, you are not doing enough." Trash. "You should wait for permission before going after what you want." Throw the whole thought away.

The real gag? You know those people who planted

those thoughts in you? Half of them do not even follow their own advice. The same family member who told you not to take risks? Probably made some wild decisions in their day. The person who told you you were not smart enough? They likely have their own regrets about not trying harder. So why are you carrying their baggage? Their lack of ability to actualize their own potential is their responsibility. It is not your job to take accountability for that. It is theirs.

Here's what happens when you don't challenge your thoughts: you stay stuck. You end up living a life designed by someone else's fears, someone else's limitations, someone else's outdated playbook. And you wake up one day wondering why you feel unfulfilled, why your life looks nothing like the one you dreamed of as a child when you were still limitless.

Consider this your permission to declutter your mind, just as you would an overstuffed closet. Pick up each thought, hold it in your hands, and ask, "Does this serve me?" If the answer is no, toss it. It is trash. If it makes you feel small, if it dims your light, if it makes you second-guess your greatness, it belongs in the landfill, not your mind.

You are powerful beyond measure. Your mind is a kingdom, and your thoughts should be fit for royalty. Not every idea deserves a throne in your head. So, next time a thought pops up telling you you cannot do something, you are not enough of something, or you do not deserve what you want, challenge it. Laugh at it if you must. And then send it straight where it belongs: in the trash.

You are not here to live a life dictated by unchecked

thoughts. You are here to create, to expand, to glow up in ways that would leave your past self in awe. But first, you have to clear out the junk.

Determining whether your thoughts are true or trash is an art, a skill, and, quite honestly, a survival tactic. If you do not question your own thoughts, who will? You would not let some random person off the street come into your house and start rearranging your furniture, so why are you letting unchecked thoughts run wild in your mind like they pay rent?

Nia had always wanted to start a YouTube channel, but every time she thought about it, her brain said, "Who do you think you are?" Instead of questioning it, she just nodded along like her brain was a wise elder rather than an over-caffeinated raccoon rifling through garbage. Meanwhile, she hyped up her friend for starting a channel, telling her, "Yaass girl, you got this!" But when it came to herself? Silence. She deserved the same energy she gave others, but for some reason, she could not extend it to herself.

Dante faced a similar mental struggle. He wanted to apply for a promotion, but his brain said, "You are not leadership material." Instead of challenging it, he simply believed it. The actual evidence? He had trained half the office; people always came to him for advice, and he basically ran the place without the title. But he never questioned it.

Aaliyah had always dreamed of moving to another city, but every time she considered it, her brain conjured up a warning: "You will not make it there." Instead of asking if that was true, she just accepted it as fact, as if there was a National Bureau of Reality that issued the judgment. The truth was that she had moved to college and thrived. She had started over in new jobs and figured it out every time. But because she never asked herself, "Is this trash?" she let a make-believe story dictate her decisions.

Then there was Malik, who loved to dance but stopped the day his dad told him, "Real men do not dance." He carried that thought with him for years, letting it harden into something that felt like a universal truth. Fast-forward twenty years: he was at a wedding, watching everyone else have the time of their lives while he stayed seated like his chair was glued to him. That belief, that dancing was not for him, did not belong to him. It was just a hand-me-down opinion from someone else's insecurities.

So, how do you take out the mental trash? Start by writing your thoughts down and putting them on trial. You are now the judge, jury, and executioner of your thoughts. If your brain tells you, "You are not good enough," ask it for qualified proof. If your thoughts insist, "You will never succeed," demand the receipts. Turn those limiting thoughts on their head. If you find yourself thinking, "I cannot do this," counter with, "What if I can?" And if your mind tells you, "I am not good enough," challenge it with, "What makes me believe that?" Your thoughts need to fight for their place in your head. Do they deserve a seat on the throne?

When you're throwing out a thought, replace it with

something better. You don't just get rid of an old couch and leave an empty space; you get a new one to fill the gap. Swap "I am not creative" for "I am creative in ways I have not explored yet." Or go nuclear and replace "I am not successful" with "And who is going to stop me?" Actively choose your thoughts the way you would curate a playlist. Right now, you might have some questionable tracks on repeat. It's time to swap them out for something better.

The biggest glow-up is not just about changing what you think. It is about reclaiming the right to think for yourself. No more recycling outdated, fear-based, hand-me-down thoughts. No more living by programs you did not write. The next time an old, limiting thought pops up, ask yourself, "Is this true, or is this trash?" And if it is trash? Toss it out, because garbage day is on Tuesday.

the thought audit

Before you can question your thoughts, you need to identify them. Many limiting beliefs operate on autopilot. It is time to bring them to the surface.

1. Take out a notebook or open a blank document.
2. Write down ten thoughts you have about yourself, money, success, love, or any area where you struggle.
3. Go through each one and ask yourself:
   - Where did this thought come from?
   - Who told me this?

- Do I actually believe this, or was it given to me?
- Has this thought helped or harmed me?
- Would I say this to a friend?
4. Now, make your judgment.

Example:

- Thought: I am not good enough to start my business.
- Source: My high school teacher always said I was a procrastinator.
- Truth: That was one class, one moment in time, and it does not define me now.
- Verdict: Trash.

the truth test

Just because a thought pops into your head does not mean it is true. You must fact-check your thoughts. When you notice yourself experiencing a negative thought, run it through these five questions:

1. Is this 100% true, with real evidence?
2. Can I think of at least one counterexample that proves it wrong?
3. If my best friend had this thought, would I agree with them?
4. What is a more empowering alternative to this thought?
5. Who benefits from my believing this thought?

Example:

- Thought: I am not good enough to get that job.
- Counterexample: I have experience and have helped my team succeed in the past.
- A more empowering thought: I am qualified and capable, and I can learn whatever I need.
- Verdict: Trash.

the "would you bet on it?" challenge

Sometimes, your brain feeds you irrational fears disguised as facts. This will help you separate fear from reality.

1. Take a fear-based thought.
2. Ask yourself, "Would I bet $1,000 that this thought is true?"
3. If you hesitate, the thought is likely not a fact, just a fear.

Example:

- Thought: I will embarrass myself if I post this video.
- Would I bet money on this happening? Probably not.
- New thought: Some people will like it, and some will not, but I will not know unless I try.
- Verdict: Trash

reverse advice

You give great advice to friends, right? It is time to give yourself that same energy.

1. Imagine your best friend has your limiting beliefs.
2. What advice would you give them?
3. Now, give that advice to yourself.

Example:

- Thought: I am not good enough to be a leader.
- The advice I would give a friend: You have been leading informally for years. Leadership is a skill that grows with experience.
- New thought: I can step into leadership by owning my strengths and learning as I go.
- Verdict: Trash.

the "talk back" method

You are not your thoughts, so talk back to them. Argue with them if you must. When a limiting thought pops up, respond with:

1. " Says who?"
2. " Prove it."
3. "And who is going to stop me, boo?"
4. "That is cute. Here is the new belief…"

Example:

- Thought: I do not deserve success.
- Response: "And who is going to stop me, boo? I define my worth."
- Verdict: Trash.

Thoughts are elusive things. They lurk in the quiet corners of your mind, shaping your reality without you even noticing. Some are helpful by pushing you forward and reminding you of your strengths. Others are nothing more than secondhand doubts—hand-me-down fears from people who never questioned their own limitations. The difference between those who change and those who stay stuck is not talent, nor is it luck or fate. It is the ability to challenge the stories they tell themselves.

Will you continue carrying the weight of thoughts that do not serve you, or will you finally put them down? Will you allow a passing doubt to dictate your future, or will you call it out for what it is? An opinion, not a fact.

The moment you question a belief, you loosen its hold on you. The moment you refuse to accept a thought as law, you reclaim your power. Every extraordinary person you admire has, at some point, stood at the edge of doubt. They have heard the same voices that tell you, "You are not good enough," "This is not for you," "You do not have what it takes." The difference? They did not take those thoughts at face value. They pushed back, challenged them, and replaced them with something better. And in doing so, they created a new reality for themselves—one that aligned with their next-level vision, not their deepest fears.

The next time a thought tells you who you are and it does not serve you, let it go. Toss it out with the same certainty as tossing out trash on a Tuesday morning. Because at the end of the day, your thoughts do not own you. You own them.

---

glow-up activation: trashing your beliefs

Pick a belief that has shaped your life, such as "I am not worthy of success" or "Money is hard to come by." Stand in front of a mirror and say this belief out loud with strong conviction. Allow yourself to feel how unpleasant it is to own and proclaim such a limiting belief. It feels unpleasant because it is not true. Now, consciously disrupt this belief by changing your body language. Stand tall, open your posture, speak louder, and add a confident tone to your voice. As you do this, notice how your body and mind react.

Write down the contradictions to this belief. For example, if the belief is "Money is hard to come by," write down instances where money has flowed into your life easily, even if only in small amounts. Over the course of a week, each time you catch yourself thinking the limiting belief, stand in front of the mirror and repeat your new belief while embodying confidence. Notice the shift in your body and energy.

the third mystic key
Reframe Your Thoughts

MOST LIKELY, you are seeing the illusion behind your thoughts, not the actual thoughts themselves. You see, there is the thought on its own, and then there is the fiction that surrounds the thought that we create. We have a tendency to make the thought mean something, as opposed to acknowledging that a thought is simply that—a thought. And not all thoughts are facts. Actually, most of them are false facts that we mistake and adopt as universal truths. The next thing you know, we have produced an award-winning apocalyptic film in our minds due to one unpleasant thought and have convinced ourselves that the world is now ending. This is the illusion behind the thought. Cinematic, right?

You are a master at flipping the script, but up until this point, you have been flipping it in the wrong direction, turning the thought into something destructive as opposed to something productive. We are now going to make it productive.

Let us set the scene. Here you are, standing at the crossroads of your mind, staring down a thought that has just waltzed in. It is loud, and it is uninvited. Maybe it's something small, like an offhand comment from your boss or a side-eye from a stranger at the grocery store. Perhaps that guy named Jared you were dating is taking too long to text you back. And before you know it, your brain has cracked its knuckles, stretched its legs, and said, "Oh, I am about to crash out." And with your eye now twitching from hysteria, what a crash out it was.

Your boss's neutral tone suddenly morphs into, "They hate me," "I am getting fired," "I am about to be homeless," and "Now I will have to busk on the subway for tips." That stranger in the grocery store? Clearly, they've recognized you from your past life as a medieval queen, and they're here to exact revenge because you beheaded them previously for heresy. And that guy Jared's delayed text? Obviously, he's drafting a long message explaining why he no longer wants you in his life, complete with bullet points.

Do you see what just happened here? One simple thought entered your mind, and instead of letting it exist as a standalone moment, you wrapped it in layers of unnecessary, fictional chaos and illusion. Not only did you just flip the script, you flipped it, lit a match, and set it on fire while smugly saying to yourself, "I knew it."

Thoughts are not facts; they are suggestions. At best, they are drafts of an idea, but under no circumstances are they the final version. The problem arises when we accept every passing thought as truth while acting as if our minds are incapable of error. If our minds were always right, we would all be billionaires with rock-hard abs and a deep sense of inner peace. Clearly, that is not the case.

Reframing your thoughts means catching them before they go full Hollywood blockbuster. It means looking at a thought and saying, "I see what you're trying to do here, but I am not letting you hijack my peace today." It means flipping the script in a way that serves you rather than sabotages you. And then putting the match down.

Imagine you're on a date, sitting across from someone who looks like they were chiseled out of stone by the gods themselves, and suddenly, they check their phone. Your brain immediately kicks into overdrive. "Oh no. They are bored." "They are probably texting their best friend right now, saying, 'Help, get me out of here.'" Before you even finish your meal, you have convinced yourself that not only are you unlovable and unattractive, but you are also destined for eternal loneliness and singledom.

But what if you reframed that thought? What if, instead of assuming the worst, you thought to yourself, "Maybe they got a text from their mom?" "Maybe they are checking the time?" "Maybe they were nervous and needed a second to breathe." See how that changes everything? One version of the story leaves you spiraling, while the other allows you to remain present and enjoy your night.

Or let's say you're at work, and your boss sends you an email with the words "Do you have a sec?" in the subject line. Now, a reasonable person would assume that it was a simple meeting. But your mind? Your mind is already composing your resignation letter because you would be damned if they beat you to it. You are now calculating unemployment and wondering how you will explain to your family that you have decided to become a nomadic goat herder in the mountains somewhere. By the time you actually step into the meeting, you are sweating, your heart is pounding, and your mind has already planned your dramatic exit speech. And what does your boss say? "Hey, just wanted to see if you would be interested in leading a new project."

See? Although it was cinematic, all of that drama was unnecessary. But you believed the illusion behind the thought instead of questioning it. You accepted the worst-case scenario without even considering the possibility of a best-case one.

Now, I am not saying you have to turn every thought into a sunshine-and-rainbows scenario. If your gut is telling you something is not right, listen to it. But do not let your gut be confused with your anxiety or your overactive imagination.

Reframing your thoughts is not about lying to yourself; it is about choosing perspectives that serve you and understanding that your brain is a storyteller and you have the power to be the editor. If your current narrative is bringing you stress, fear, or unnecessary chaos, you have every right to go back, hit the delete key, and write a better one.

The mind is an incredible tool, but like any tool, it needs direction. Left unchecked, it will build unnecessary walls, dig holes where there should be bridges, and convince you that a minor inconvenience is a lifelong catastrophe. However, when guided and given clear instructions, the mind will work in your favor. It will help you see opportunities where there once were obstacles and solutions where there once were problems.

Reframing your thoughts is an art. It is the moment you catch your mind weaving its web of lies and decide, "Actually, I am not going to do this today." It is the difference between believing your thoughts at face value and realizing, "Hold up, I am literally making this up as I go."

Reframing is about learning to disrupt that automatic reaction before it has the opportunity to take over. It is about recognizing that thoughts are just thoughts. Not universal truths, not prophecies, and certainly not reality unless you let them be.

You have already challenged your thoughts. You have questioned their origins and dissected their logic by pulling them out into the light, exposing their flaws. You have realized that so many of them were never truly yours to begin with. But knowing that a thought is untrue does not automatically erase it. It lingers and still hums in the background. It still shapes the way you feel, the way you move, and the way you see yourself.

Reframing is not just about thinking positively. It is about taking full control over your mind by reshaping your internal narrative and deciding with conviction what story you will tell about yourself and your life. It is the conscious, deliberate act of replacing an old thought with a new, more empowering one. It is the difference between seeing yourself as a victim of circumstance and recognizing yourself as the author of your own experience. Your thoughts don't just describe reality; they create it.

A frame gives meaning to a picture. The same image, placed in a different frame, can evoke an entirely different feeling. A cheap plastic frame makes it seem ordinary and forgettable, while a gilded, ornate frame turns it into something worthy of admiration. The picture itself has not changed, only the way it is presented.

Your mind does this automatically. It frames every experience, every event, and every interaction according to the beliefs and assumptions you have internalized. If you have been conditioned to see yourself as someone who always falls short, then every setback becomes further proof of your inadequacy. If you believe that the universe is against you, then every challenge feels like an attack rather than an opportunity.

But what happens if you change the frame?

What happens if you take the same event and shift the perspective? Suddenly, failure is no longer failure; it is feedback. Rejection is no longer proof that you are unworthy; it is redirection to something better. A painful past is not just a series of wounds; it is now the foundation of your wisdom, resilience, and strength. The moment you change the frame, you change the story.

To reframe your thoughts, you must actively rewrite the script playing in your mind. This is not about ignoring reality or pretending that everything is perfect.

It is about choosing an interpretation that empowers you rather than limits you.

identify the thought you want to reframe

You already know the thought is unhelpful, but now, you have to decide how you want to change it. The key is specificity. The more clearly you define the thought, the easier it is to rewrite it.

For example, instead of saying, "I always fail," you boil it down:

1. "I failed at launching my business the first time."
2. "I did not get the job I wanted."
3. "My last relationship did not work out."

Once you get specific, the thought loses its sweeping, all-encompassing power. You stop making it about your entire identity and start seeing it as a single experience that can be reinterpreted.

ask, "what else could be true?"

The mistake most people make is assuming their initial interpretation is the only valid one. It is not. It is just the most familiar one. But the mind, when directed, is capable of offering infinite perspectives.

So ask yourself, "What else could be true about this situation?"

1. Instead of saying, "I failed at launching my business the first time." What if the truth is that "I learned exactly what does not work, so my next attempt will be stronger"?
2. Instead of saying, "I did not get the job I wanted." What if the truth is "That job was not aligned with my next-level version, and something better is waiting for me"?
3. Instead of saying, "My last relationship did not work out." What if the truth is "That relationship taught me what I need and deserve, making me wiser for the next one"?

This step is not about forcing yourself to believe something unrealistic. It is about acknowledging that multiple things can be true at one time and choosing the one that serves you best.

embody the new thought

Knowing the reframe is one thing, but living the reframe is another. Your brain has spent years strengthening neural pathways that reinforce old thoughts and belief systems. Reframing requires building new pathways, and that takes repetition.

Each time the old thought tries to creep back in, do not fight it. Instead, redirect it. Imagine your mind as a radio station. When static comes through (the old thought), you do not panic. You simply adjust the dial. Send it back into space. Or knock it out with a mallet like a whack-a-mole.

So, when the thought, "I am not good enough,"

arises, do not argue with it. Just replace it with, "I am constantly growing and evolving." When the thought, "Nothing ever works out for me," surfaces, adjust the dial to, "I am being guided to something greater than I can currently see." The more you do this, the weaker the old thought becomes. Your brain is adaptable. It will follow the direction you give it, but you have to be consistent.

———

Your life is shaped by the stories you tell yourself. Every belief you hold, every assumption you make, and every decision you make all stem from the internal narrative running in your mind. Most people do not realize they are living inside a story they did not even write. They are carrying beliefs passed down from family, society, and past experiences without ever questioning if they are true. But once you understand that your mind is a storyteller, you gain the power to edit the script.

You do not have to keep telling the story of failure, struggle, and limitation. You do not have to keep replaying the same tired narratives that keep you small. You can decide, at any moment, to tell a different story. A story where you are capable. A story where you are worthy. A story where every challenge is a stepping stone rather than a roadblock. Because no matter what you tell yourself, *your mind will believe you.*

So, pick up the pen, flip the script, and write a new story. And this time, you'd better make it one that is worth living.

glow-up activation: flipping the script

In your journal, write out the most negative story you have been telling yourself about who you are or what your life is. This could be a narrative about your worth, your potential, your success, or your relationships. It should be the one you have felt stuck in for the longest. Do not hold back or sugarcoat it. Be brutally honest and write it out as vividly and dramatically as possible. If your story is that you will never succeed in your career, write it in a way that amplifies that fear. If it is about relationships, bring in all the hopelessness. Let it be a dark narrative.

Once you have written out the negative version of your story, read it aloud to yourself, and as you are reading it, imagine that this version of your story is someone else's life. Imagine it is a character in a book or a movie.

When you are done reading, ask yourself, "How does this story make me feel about this person? What advice would I give them?" Write that advice in your journal as if you are speaking to that character from the outside. What would you say to this person to help them flip their script? Now, tell yourself that.

the fourth mystic key

Shift the Vibe

UP UNTIL THIS POINT, you have addressed your individual thoughts and begun forming new ones. These new ones now need to be brought together to form the new belief system. This process requires bringing it all together into a new, cohesive system that you resonate with and feel a connection to, which will not only make it easier to adhere to your new mindset but will also help complete the transformation of your mind.

Without bringing it all together, there is no deliberate attempt to solidify the new belief system, and we have all seen how quickly it can fall apart after that. Have you ever committed to being extra healthy and fit for a New Year's resolution? Maybe you decided to cut out sugar and start going to the gym. And you really believed it, too! The next thing you know, it is February, and you are wearing your buffet pants to the dinner table to "make room."

At first, this change will feel like a spark or a

moment of clarity, a newfound excitement that washes over you. You will start seeing things differently, catching yourself in old habits, and replacing them with better ones. You have been doing the work. You have examined your thoughts, sifted through the rubble of your limiting beliefs, and begun crafting new ones. At this point, it might feel like you are on the cusp of something big, as if you can actually feel your future self within reach, just waiting for you to step fully into your next-level version.

But the problem is, if you do not bring all of these new thoughts together into a solid, cohesive belief system, that next-level version of you will remain just out of reach. You will keep bouncing back and forth between your old and new ways of thinking, never fully landing on either. One day, you will feel powerful and assured; the next day, you will find yourself slipping into the same doubts, the same habits, and the same vibe that got you stuck in the first place. And then, without even realizing it, you are right back where you started, wondering if you ever really changed at all.

This is why shifting your vibe by bringing all your new thoughts into a solid, cohesive belief system is the fourth key to changing your thinking. Because mindset is not just a collection of thoughts; it is the environment those thoughts live in. It is the foundation. And if you do not build that foundation strong enough, your new thoughts will collapse under the weight of your old conditioning the moment you stop paying attention.

You have probably been here before. Maybe it was that time you decided to stop procrastinating and finally get serious about your goals. You bought a planner, wrote out a schedule, and even blocked out time on your calendar. For the first two weeks, you were on fire, checking things off your list, staying focused, and feeling unstoppable. Then, one day, you were tired, and you skipped a task. "I will make up for it tomorrow," you told yourself. But tomorrow came, and you were still tired, so you pushed it back again. Before you knew it, the planner was buried under a pile of unopened mail, and your schedule was just a list of things you kept rescheduling. At that moment, you wondered, "Did I really change at all?"

Or maybe it was a relationship. You promised yourself you would not go back to that one ex, the one who had you questioning your self-worth and who never quite showed up the way you needed. You were doing great at first, clear, focused, and standing firm in your boundaries. Then, a lonely night hit. A "Hey, you" text slid into your messages, and before you could think twice, you were right back in it. Why? Because while you may have thought to move on, you had not fully shifted into your new belief system. You were still operating under old programming, still resonating with the same frequency that attracted that dynamic in the first place.

Your mind and your energy will always default to the strongest system in place. If the strongest system is your old way of thinking, that is what you will fall back on. If the strongest system is your new mindset, then that is what will hold. This is why shifting your vibe by fully integrating these new thoughts into a rock-solid belief system is non-negotiable. It is what turns change from something temporary into something permanent.

Imagine your mind is a house. Your old belief system is the foundation it was built on, and right now, your new thoughts are simply decoration. Like new, fresh, stylish furniture you just brought in to brighten up the space. Now, if that foundation is cracked and weak, what is going to happen? That beautiful new furniture will not mean anything if the house collapses. Everything will crumble the moment the first storm comes along during hurricane season. You will go right back to the old structure, the one you were trying to leave behind in the first place.

This is why just thinking new thoughts is not enough. You have to live them. You have to become them. You have to build an entire internal world where these thoughts do not just exist but thrive. And that starts with making a choice. Not just a half-hearted, "I will try" kind of choice, but a full-bodied, unwavering, "I am not available for anything less than this" kind of choice.

When you truly shift your vibe, you will notice something wild happen. The things that used to tempt you? They will no longer register the same way anymore. The fears that used to hold you back? They will lose their grip. And the doubts that used to creep in? They will not carry the same weight that they used to, because you will have become someone who no longer entertains those things anymore. Not out of effort, but because they simply do not match your new reality.

It is like upgrading your internal frequency. If you

have ever tuned a radio, you know that each station has a specific frequency. If you are tuned into static, it doesn't matter how much you want to hear music; you're not on the right channel. But the second you adjust the dial, suddenly, the music is clear. The same goes for your mind. You cannot just want to change. You have to shift the whole damn station.

Shifting your vibe requires a full, energetic change, not just an intellectual one. It is about what you allow yourself to accept as reality. The reason why new thoughts do not always stick is that they are still in competition with the old ones. If your old belief system has been built over the years or even decades, it becomes like an old house that you have been living in forever. You know its creaky floors, the spots where the paint is chipped, and the way the door sticks when it is humid outside. Even if it's not the house you want, it's familiar. Your new belief system is like the brand-new house you're trying to move into, but you haven't yet set up all the furniture or figured out how the new dishwasher works. It does not feel like home yet.

This is why, even after you decide to change, you sometimes feel that pull back toward the old version of you. It is why, even when you commit to believing in yourself, you still hear that inner voice saying, "But what if this is not real?" It's because you haven't made your new thoughts feel like home yet.

To shift your vibe completely, you have to surround yourself with evidence that supports your new reality. Your environment plays a significant role in shaping your beliefs, and if everything around you is reinforcing the old story, you are going to struggle to anchor into the new one. This is not just about external things like the people you talk to or the content you consume (although those matter, too). It is about what you mentally allow yourself to accept as truth. If you are still listening to your doubts as if they have authority over you, then you are giving them a seat at the table. They might not be cooking the dinner, but they are still eating.

The way to solidify your new belief system is to make it non-negotiable. You have to flood your mind with reinforcement. This means choosing to engage only with the thoughts that align with your new reality. Every time an old thought arises, you meet it with a firm, "That is not me anymore." You redirect. You slap it down. You become relentless about reinforcing the new way of thinking until it becomes second nature. It is not enough to think new thoughts occasionally. You have to make them the dominant voice in your mind. You have to let them become the loudest, most familiar thing you hear. You have to allow yourself to become the most familiar thing you hear.

And something most people may not realize is that shifting your vibe does not always feel good at first. Sometimes, it feels uncomfortable or awkward. Maybe even unnatural. That is because you are doing something new. If you have spent a lifetime doubting yourself, confidence is going to make you feel like a fraud at first. If you have spent a lifetime expecting things to go wrong, trusting that things will go right is going to feel like a lie. That discomfort does not mean you are doing it wrong; it means you are changing. At first, the new way of thinking takes effort. It requires conscious awareness. But eventually, it becomes your natural state, and the old way of thinking starts to feel out of place.

You also need to eliminate contradictions. If you are telling yourself that you are going to be your next-level version by stepping into a new mindset but still engaging in things that reinforce the old one, you are creating internal conflict. You cannot fully shift into self-belief while still indulging in your fits of self-doubt. You cannot claim to be someone who follows through while still giving yourself permission to quit because you got scared and something felt hard. Your actions, your thoughts, and your energy all have to line up. Every time you let a contradictory thought or behavior slide, you weaken the foundation of your new belief system. Remember, your new beliefs are non-negotiable.

This is why you have to get clear on what you actually believe now. Decide that your new truth is that "I always figure things out," because then that has to be the answer every time doubt creeps in. If your new truth is that "I am already successful," then you do not entertain thoughts of unworthiness because they are trash. It is about making a choice—a firm, non-negotiable choice about what you will and will not accept for your life anymore.

You do not have to wait for permission or proof to believe something new, and you do not have to wait for anything outside of you to confirm it. You decide. And once you decide, you let everything else adjust to that decision. Why? Because you have been adjusting to everyone else and everything else your whole life. You already paid your dues, and it is now time for the world to adjust to you. When you fully commit to the new way of thinking, the world around you starts responding to you differently. The things that used to trigger you just do not hit the same. You will start attracting different experiences, different people, and different opportunities. Not because something external has changed, but because *you* have shifted.

how to shift the vibe permanently

To shift your vibe permanently, you need to anchor it into your daily life. Here is how:

1. **Reset Your Space.** Start by looking at your physical space. What is in it that reinforces old beliefs? Clear out objects, books, photos, or even furniture that connect you to an old way of thinking. Change your surroundings to reflect the next-level version of yourself you are stepping into. This could mean redecorating your living space or simply removing clutter, which is energetic stagnation.
2. **Peep Your Inner Voice.** Pay attention to how you talk to yourself. Each time an old belief creeps in, counter it immediately with the opposite thought. Say it out loud if you need to. Scream it into the ethers. Record voice notes of yourself speaking your new beliefs and listen to them daily.
3. **Cut the Contradictions.** If your new belief is that you are disciplined, stop engaging in

behaviors that reinforce inconsistency. If you claim to be confident, stop entertaining self-hate speech. Every action should support the identity you are stepping into. Hold yourself accountable and notice when you are allowing old habits to creep back in. If you do not do it, no one else will.
4. **Reinforce It.** Surround yourself with content that supports your new mindset. Read books, listen to podcasts, and engage in conversations that align with who you are *now*.
5. **Relentless Repetition.** Your mind rewires through repetition. Make a habit of reaffirming your new beliefs multiple times a day. I do not care if you journal about them, speak them out loud, or think about them. Over time, these beliefs will become your automatic way of thinking and naturally replace the old ones.

Shifting your vibe is about aligning your internal world so completely that your external reality has no choice but to follow. Notice that I did not say that you must align *with* your internal world. You align your internal world by telling it what to do in the same way a teacher tells a kindergarten class to line up for lunch.

It's not just about changing your thoughts; it's about establishing a new internal standard for what you accept as true. You are creating boundaries with yourself. The strongest belief always wins, and it is survival of the fittest. When your new mindset is fully integrated, it stops being a struggle and starts being who you are.

You will know the shift is real when you no longer feel the need to convince yourself. The doubts will not disappear overnight, but they will lose their grip and fade out of significance. The thoughts that once pulled you back will feel out of touch, like your old Grandpa Joe, who still has not figured out that some things are just inappropriate to say at the dinner table. You will not have to force yourself to stay on track because your new mindset will be the only reality that makes sense.

―――――

glow-up activation: shifting the vibe

Write down every single thought you have that is holding you back from your next-level life. These are the thoughts that come up when you feel insecure, unworthy, stuck, or afraid. Let the raw, unfiltered thoughts spill onto the page. This is the old story you have been telling yourself.

Now, take each belief and completely obliterate it. I am talking about shattering it, breaking it apart, and writing a new narrative as if you are God, rewriting the story of your life. If you wrote, "I feel like a failure," rewrite it as, "I am destined for greatness. Success is inevitable, and I am a force of nature in everything I do."

Immediately after you have spoken your new beliefs, take ONE action that aligns with your new story to shift the vibe. Do not wait. Do not think. You need to prove to yourself that your new beliefs are true by taking bold action right now. If you declared, "I am capable of achieving my dreams," take one small, but mighty step by making the call, sending the email, or signing up for that class you have been procrastinating on.

the fifth mystic key
Move Like It

THE ERA of sitting with your passive thoughts is over. It is now time to do. Time to act. If you want reality to bend to you, you must recognize that it is you who must bend. The time of downplaying your ideas and shrinking yourself to appease others stops right now. That imposter syndrome that you have been historically using to hold yourself back? Throw that out the window.

You now have this new belief system, but you have to move with it and set it into motion. It is the spiritual equivalent of going to the gym. If you do not use it, you will lose it. You have to work out your new thought muscles to turn them into habits. Your old belief system developed by working those muscles again and again and again until they turned into a sweat-glistening bicep rippling with each movement. But your new arms, along with your new belief system, are weak. Weak like the scrawny math nerd in gym class trying to do a pull-up. It is shaky at best.

The fastest way to implement your new thoughts

and belief system to transform your reality and trigger that glow-up is to embody the version of yourself who already has what you desire. But the part that most people misunderstand is that embodiment is not just about what you do; it is about who you are being. It is not just about external action but the internal state from which you operate.

Most people try to manifest things by focusing on the outcome. They script their desires, they visualize, and they write affirmations a hundred times in their journal like they are in detention for wanting too much. Then there is this funny idea that if you think it hard enough, the manifestation will just *poof* and appear out of thin air. But the caveat? They fail to become the person who actually receives it. They are obsessed with the thing instead of the transformation required to get the thing.

What you need to understand is that you do not attract what you want. You attract what you are.

If you still see yourself as the person struggling, as the person who "wants" but does not "have," then that is exactly what reality will reflect back to you. You will stay in a cycle of longing, hoping, and wishing because reality is always responding to your dominant frequency, not your desperate affirmations. This is why acting like you have the thing or moving like you are the thing is so important. Stop asking for what you want and start being the person who already has it.

The version of you who has already made it is not sitting around hoping the Universe finally decides to bless them. They are not waiting for a sign. They do not hesitate when making every decision. They have already decided who and what they are. They live in the energy of *done*. And that is what the Law of Embodiment requires. It demands that you stop *trying* and start *being*.

Let me tell you something that will set you free forever, if you let it sink in. Reality is a mirror. It is not a wish-granting vending machine. Most people operate as if reality is something separate from them, as if there is some cosmic scale in the sky weighing their worthiness and deciding if they should be rewarded.

Reality does not operate on requests. It operates on reflection. It does not "give" you what you want; it simply reflects back to you who you are being. Think about it. When you look in a mirror, you do not beg the reflection to change before you do. You do not plead with it to make you look more confident, more influential, or more worthy. If you want to see something different, you change first, and then the mirror reflects those changes back to you. If you smile, your reflection in the mirror smiles back.

Changing your thoughts and beliefs is not enough. Your energy must match it, and that is the next part of the glow-up. You must learn to embody the new identity that you have just birthed from disposing of those thought patterns that no longer serve you. The fastest way to embody is by moving accordingly.

If you want to know what you are currently embodying, look around you and see what reality is reflecting back to you. If you keep seeing lack, then that new millionaire mindset you created needs additional help to set itself into motion. If you are embodying doubt, the world will reflect doubt. If you are embodying struggle by holding on to the remnants of your "life is hard" belief system, the world will reflect struggle. If you embody hesitation, the world will reflect hesitation. But the moment you embody self-assuredness, being sure of your new thoughts and beliefs, reality will start to bend in your favor.

Most people wait for a signal before they move. They want confirmation that they are on the right path before they fully commit. They want to see proof before they invest their energy. But what signal do you need when you have already decided on your new reality? You have already gone through the process of reshaping your thinking in order to get what you want, so do not add an extra, unnecessary step to the process. Reality will not bend to your hesitancy because you are not sure yet.

The powerless do not have a need for a glow-up, but those who are harnessing their inner power? They do. The ones who truly shape reality do not wait for validation or permission. You do not have time for the outside world to catch up when it took you this long to catch up to yourself. You have already done the work to decide who you are or who you want to be, so just do it. Because reality does not respond to passive energy seeping with hesitation and insecurity. It bends to certainty. To a choice that was made firmly.

This is why some people can walk into a room and command attention without saying a word. There is just something about them that makes you turn your head and look. It is not because they are special or lucky. It is because they are moving without hesitation. Their energy is already in a state of arrival, so naturally, when they arrive, you notice them.

That is what embodiment is. It is moving as if. Not pretending or faking it, but stepping fully into the truth that is already yours. If you are waiting for the world to validate your transformation before you embody it, you will be waiting forever. You must embody it first, and then the world will adjust accordingly. Reality will bend.

This process is about remembering who you were before you were convinced otherwise. Embodiment is not about changing into something new or pretending to be what you are not; it is about reclaiming what has always been yours through the process of stripping away every false identity, every limitation, every doubt, and stepping fully into the power that was never actually lost, just forgotten.

You are here to glow up into your next-level version because, deep down, you know there is something on the side that has been waiting for you to catch up to it. You are the next-level version, and the world does not need more next-levels waiting for permission. The world does not need more next-levels waiting to gain some confidence. The world does not need more next-levels shrinking themselves because they are afraid to be seen.

The world needs next-level people who own themselves fully. The world needs next-level people who step into their power without hesitation. The world needs you moving like it, embodying it, living it.

Because the moment you decide that you are already the thing, the moment you hold that truth so deeply that reality has no choice but to reflect it back, that is when the glow-up becomes more than just a possibility. It is now inevitable.

And let me tell you what not to do. Do not be that person who hypes themselves up in the mirror, struts out the door with a Beyoncé-level walk, and then immediately shrinks the second someone asks you a challenging question. Do not be the person who says, "This is my year. I am unstoppable!" and then stops at the first inconvenience.

How many times have you almost embodied your new reality? You were right there, so close. You walked into the meeting with the energy of a CEO, ready to command the room, and then, the moment someone disagreed with you, you shrank into the intern version of yourself. You were about to say no to something that did not serve you, and then the fear of disappointing people had you out here saying, "Oh, it is fine! No worries!" while your soul screamed. You were going to launch the thing, post the video, and step into your power, but then you hesitated, overthought it, and suddenly, you're scrolling on your phone, convincing yourself that you'll do it tomorrow. Lies.

See the pattern? Almost is not enough. Embodiment requires follow-through.

I see you. You are nodding along, feeling the energy of these words, but there is still that one lingering question that I know is in the back of your mind. *Okay, I heard you, Mystic Rainn, but how do I actually do this? How do I move like it?*

I got you.

Moving like it is not about faking it until you make it. It is about being it until you become it. It's about embodying your new belief system right now, rather than waiting for external confirmation that you are "ready." If you wait for the world to give you the green light, you are going to spend the rest of your life sitting at a red light, watching everyone else speed through the intersection.

Here is exactly how you start moving like it:

move like it in your mind

Before any external action happens, you have to get your mind on board.

1. Catch yourself when your thoughts contradict your new belief system. If you think, "I do not know if I am good enough," immediately replace it with, "I am already more than enough."
2. If your brain starts spiraling into self-doubt, stop the thought mid-sentence. Do not entertain it. Remember to challenge your beliefs. Is it true? Or is it trash?
3. Validate yourself. Look at yourself in the mirror and say, "I am successful, I am powerful, and the world adjusts to me." And

if it feels weird, good. That means you are stepping into something new.

Your mind is a muscle, and every thought is a rep. Strengthen it.

move like it in your body

Your body speaks before you do. If you walk into a room hunched over, hesitant, eyes darting around to see if you "belong," guess what? You are telling the world (and yourself) that you do not belong in that space.

Instead:

1. **Adjust your posture.** Shoulders back. Chin up, buttercup. Move like you take up space—because you do.
2. **Slow down.** Confident people do not rush. They move with intention. They enter rooms like they belong, not like they need to explain why they are there.
3. **Use your voice.** Speak up. Speak clearly. No more trailing off at the end of sentences or shrinking your volume.

Confidence is felt before it is heard. Your body is your first language, so make sure it is saying the right thing.

move like it in your decisions

A lot of people wait until they *feel* like the person they want to be before they start making moves. Can I let you in on a secret? Not only is that thinking backward, but it is also an illusion. The only way you become that person is by making decisions as if you already are. You will not miraculously wake up on a beautiful morning with that feeling. You must shift into the feeling by embodying it.

So, ask yourself:

1. Would the successful, next-level version of me say yes to this opportunity?
2. Would the next-level version of me, who already has the life I want, hesitate right now?
3. What decision would I make if I were already where I wanted to be?

Then do that. Not later. Now. Every decision is a declaration. Choose like the next-level version of you who has already done the work to change their thinking, because you have.

move like it in your daily actions

The small things matter. Moving like it is not just about grand gestures; it is also about how you carry yourself in the mundane moments.

1. How does the next-level version of you wake up in the morning?
2. How does the next-level version of you respond to setbacks?
3. How does the next-level version of you take care of themselves?

Start acting as if you are already that person, and eventually, you will not be acting. You will just be. Do not forget that you are forming new habits to fit your new thoughts and beliefs.

move like it in your energy

Energy is everything, and it is the only thing the Universe responds to. If you want your reality to bend, you must first check your energy. It is the difference between two people saying the same words, but one of them is compelling, and the other one is forgettable. Your days of being forgettable are over.

1. **Check your energy before you enter a room.** Are you walking in with doubt or certainty?
2. **Hold your own.** Do not shrink. Do not downplay. Stand in the fullness of who you are.
3. **Own your space.** Not just physically but energetically. Your presence alone should shift the environment.

———

The Glow-Up Manifesto

Remember the secret, which is that reality does not bend to you first. You bend reality. And the moment you make this shift, everything around you will shift, too.

Moving like it is about stripping away everything that told you that you were not already iconic. It is about remembering who you were before the world told you to shrink. You do not need more signs. You do not need more reassurance. You need to decide.

What is the alternative? To keep waiting? To keep hoping someone else comes along and crowns you worthy? To keep playing small while watching other people less talented than you step into everything you know deep down is meant for you?

Absolutely not.

You have already done the work. You have already shifted your thinking. The only thing left to do is to step into it fully. No more *almosts*. No more hesitating at the threshold or waiting for someone else to confirm that you are allowed to take up space.

You do not need permission. You never did.

And the moment you embody that truth? The moment you move with the confidence of someone who explains nothing, apologizes for nothing, and shrinks for no one? That is when the glow-up is inevitable.

———

glow-up activation: the next-level self catwalk

Choose one area of your life where you want to experience immediate transformation. For example, your career, love life, or health. Close your eyes and imagine your next-level self in this area, fully embodied in the person you want to become. Now, open your eyes and physically walk as if you are that next-level self. How do you stand? How do you walk? What energy do you project to the world?

For the next 24 hours, speak the way they would speak, make decisions the way they would, and notice how others respond to your energy. Journal your experiences and take note of the differences in how you move and interact with others. What does this reveal about the power of embodying your next-level self?

the sixth mystic key
Hold Your Position

LET ME BE CLEAR. This step is mission-critical. If you do not do this step, you will risk losing all your progress. In fact, it is usually at this step where most people will pause, think they did something wrong, and so they turn around or just quit altogether. Holding your position means standing firm in your new beliefs even when you feel you are being confronted with challenges or that your life is not reflecting your new mindset.

You must lock in your new way of thinking prior to having any external validation to back up the new shifts that are happening in your life. You must resist the doubt that starts creeping in and the urge to give up just because you may feel like you lack tangible confirmation that things are changing. It is easy to be excited for what is to come, but all of the gunk needs to be cleared out first, and during the gunk-clearing phase, you will experience the "gap."

the "gap"

By the time you make it to this point, you will feel like you have fully committed to the idea. That you have worked on transforming and eliminating those outdated beliefs and thought patterns. You may even feel like you have been working extra hard at making sure your new actions are aligned with your new way of thinking.

You may have moved houses, eliminated friendships or relationships, left jobs, started a new business, and prioritized your health, all in an effort to create that next-level life that is a dream for you. You probably started off optimistic and full of enthusiasm for what was going to come for you. And then, next thing you know, you feel like you have ended up in what I like to call the "gap." The "gap" is the period of time or the part in the middle of when you have changed your mindset and when your outer reality begins to mirror what your new thinking is.

You have done the work and have followed all of the steps. Up until now, you have established your awareness, challenged your old beliefs, reframed old thoughts, changed your thinking, and taken action. And then something will happen that will make you question everything you have done and whether or not it is actually working.

During this time, your old way of living will still be in the process of fading out. It may feel as if it is lingering around too long. You will feel like, "Come on, I have changed. How long until my life changes, too?" Others may think, "Maybe I did not do something right," or "Maybe this is not working." Your life is changing, but it is finishing out that final cycle you were on prior to you making those new decisions. If you lose faith in this moment and revert to your old ways, you will stop your life from completing its shift.

The Universe has a humor to it in that, while you are in the "gap," it will use the opportunity to ask you, "Are you sure you want to change this?" We humans have a tendency to say that the Universe is "testing" us, or that we must go through a set of trials and tribulations to prove that we deserve something better. This is not true. The Universe is simply mirroring your previous patterns of thought and behavior. So, when asked if you are sure, this is happening because you have spent a lifetime doing other things. Most likely, a lifetime of making disempowered decisions has led to various situations that did not serve your highest good. The Universe is not testing you; it is being courteous by verifying your new beliefs prior to making the final shifts for your new reality because, in the past, you made different decisions.

It is easy for humans to accuse the Universe of sending tests rather than taking accountability and responsibility for their own lives. When unfortunate situations happen to you as a child, yes, you may have been helpless, but holding on to those situations well into your adulthood and using them as a reason why you cannot thrive is a disempowered way to live. Only you have the ability to decide that your life from this point forward will be made only using your own empowered decisions.

The "gap" is uncomfortable, as it is the space

between who you are now and what you are to become. After you plant a seed, there is a period in between where seemingly nothing happens until one day, a plant pops out of the soil. You have already done the work to create this new garden, and the "gap" is you waiting for the new plant to pop out. You have planted an acorn that is in the process of turning into an oak tree. So, before you give up on the whole process, just give it a minute and let things take root beneath the surface.

what is happening in the "gap"?

There is a lot going on in that soil beneath the surface, and it needs time to finalize itself, even if you feel like you can't see it.

1. **The new mind you have created is adjusting.** You have worked hard to transform your mindset and change your beliefs. You have had a certain belief pattern that you have carried for years or even since childhood. It takes time for your transformed thinking to become your new dominant, automatic way of thinking.
2. **Your environment is adjusting.** People and circumstances will start to rearrange themselves to match your new belief systems and behavior. This will look like situations or people leaving your life, or an overall "reorganization."
3. **Your actions are building momentum.** Your outgoing way of living was created due to a

pattern of behaviors established over a long period of time. These old actions have a lifetime's worth of momentum that not only needs to be stopped but, in many cases, needs to be reversed to align with your new actions. Energetically stopping that momentum is like stopping a runaway freight train. Simultaneously, during this period, your new actions are creating fresh energy and momentum to propel you in the new direction you wish to go.
4. **The Universe is asking you, "Are you sure?"** This will manifest as situations or people challenging you or making it harder for you to achieve new results, and you will feel like you are encountering resistance as you work towards your goals. You may notice that people begin to question your decisions or outright disapprove of the new path you are taking.

It is because of these reasons that self-doubt will begin to creep in before you are even aware that it exists, because the "gap" is making you feel like nothing is happening, or the opposite is happening. We live in a world that prioritizes immediate results. In a job, if you cannot produce immediate results, you are likely to be fired, and in a relationship, if you cannot produce immediate results, you are often left. It is natural to expect immediate results when you change your thinking, but because of our society, we hold the belief that if results are not immediate, we have made a mistake or have failed.

This is the hardest part of the transformation process, and when people misunderstand what is happening, this is when they quit — when they are so close to the end. This self-doubt is not a reflection of whether you have changed. It is a result of societal expectations and is simply a reminder that you are in the "gap." In fact, when self-doubt begins to creep in, there should be a sense of excitement that you have made it to the sixth Mystic Key of the process. You have nearly completed the transformation.

As you navigate the "gap," it is important to remember that this period is not just about waiting for your new reality to manifest. It is an opportunity for you to grow and consolidate your plans and expectations. At this moment, the seeds you have planted are taking root and gaining strength. You will not be able to see the progress above the surface, but beneath it in the soil, a big transformation is occurring.

Your new mindset is taking shape and solidifying, and the Universe is realigning itself to match your new thoughts and beliefs. Your old patterns and ways of thinking are being pushed out of the way for something stronger and more authentic — more you.

The "gap" is also a period of self-discovery and reflection. It is an opportunity to explore your true desires and refine your vision for the future. This is where you get to make edits and tweaks to your next-level you. As you anticipate the unfolding of your new reality, take this as an opportunity to check yourself and confirm that your actions are aligned with the version of you that you say you want to be.

The good news is that the "gap" is maneuverable. It is possible to navigate out of the gap if you have a little bit of guts. Actually, having a healthy set of balls is capable of closing the "gap" relatively quickly. It does not require an act from the Universe; it requires you to act.

I want to be clear. The way to get out of the "gap" is going to feel counterintuitive. For some of you, it may hurt. Why? Because it is going to require that you do and become the antithesis of what you were conditioned to do and who you were conditioned to become. You see, family has molded you, and society's structure has polished and refined you, turning you into a person who has historically sought external validation and permission prior to making any of your own decisions. You have been taught to believe that all great work and ideas that come from you must first be approved by some source outside of you in order for you to move on it. For some of you, that source is God; for others of you, that source is your mother.

Breaking out of the "gap" is going to require that you rebel so hard that the very act of your rebellion sparks a personal revolution. Because what happened is that you have landed in the "gap" with your fears and doubts due to previously built-up negative reinforcement that has been trickling its way into your life since childhood. Every time you got yelled at for expressing an original thought because it did not align with the status quo. Every time you were scolded for coloring on the walls, because to the

4-year-old you, that white wall looked like a blank canvas. Every time you expressed your dreams to your mother, she scoffed at them. Every time you revealed your passions to a friend, and although it was well-meaning, that friend asked, "Are you sure that is possible?"

As a child, you were full of imagination and creativity, eager to explore and express yourself. Do you remember the first time you brought home a paper plate and dried macaroni noodle creation? Beaming with pride as you presented it to your family, but instead of praise, you found your masterpiece in the trash a few days later, unnoticed and unappreciated. This was just the first of many instances where your unique thoughts and ideas were dismissed or scolded. There was the time you expressed your dreams to your mother, only to be met with skepticism and doubt. And when you shared your passions with a well-meaning friend, their question, "Are you sure that is possible?" planted a seed of self-doubt in your mind.

Every time you colored outside the lines or thought outside the box, it felt like you were doing something wrong, something that deserved punishment or ridicule. These experiences shaped your outlook and approach to life. They taught you to seek external validation and approval before taking action and to conform to the expectations of others rather than forging your own path. And now, as an adult, you find yourself in the "gap," that uncomfortable space between who you are and who you want to be. It is true that it is a place of self-doubt and uncertainty, but it is also an opportunity for growth and transformation.

To navigate out of the "gap," you must find the

audacity to rebel against the conditioning that has held you back. It will not be easy, but it is necessary to break free from the limitations imposed on you by others.

breaking out of the "gap"

You did not come this far just to quit now. The "gap" is not a roadblock; it is your final opportunity to confirm to the Universe that you will do the thing you said you were going to do and be the person you said you were going to be. This is not the time to crumble under the weight of old programming. You are being pushed to step into your next-level self. And make no mistake, the only way out at this point is moving forward. If you try to retreat, you will only end up stuck in the same cycle of doubt, fear, and hesitation.

Do you want to break out of the "gap"? Break the version of yourself that still believes you need permission to be great. Here's how:

1. **Burn the bridge back to who you used to be**. You cannot afford to keep one foot in your old life while reaching for the new one. You must cut off all exits that lead back to your comfort zone. Your old self, that part of you that hesitates, asks for permission, and shrinks to make others comfortable, is dead. Stop entertaining the possibility of failure. Stop "waiting for a sign." Stop looking for reassurance. Decide right now that there is no way back. You are already on the other side. Remember to act like it.

2. **Make a ruthless, unapologetic decision.** The gap exists because you have not made a final decision to own your new reality. You are wobbling, questioning your choices, and hesitating. Indecision is a curse that you place upon yourself. It keeps you trapped in a loop of "almost" and "not yet." The moment you make a non-negotiable decision, the gap begins to close. Decide right now that your transformation is happening, and nothing—not fear, not doubt, not other people's opinions—can stop it.
3. **Move while you are still afraid.** Fear will not leave if you are sitting and overthinking. You must move through it. The lie you have been told is that clarity comes *before* action. It does not. Clarity comes *from* action. The more you move, the more certain you become. Right now, your brain is programmed to hesitate because it has been trained to seek safety over expansion. Your job is to override that conditioning by moving before your mind catches up.
4. **Rebel a little.** The version of you that seeks permission and approval is not the real you; it is a construct created by a lifetime of conditioning. Your family dynamics and societal culture made you this way, but you are too great to hesitate. To break out of the gap, you must rebel against the forces that tamed you. Every time you move, you are committing an act of personal revolution.

Your growth is an act of defiance against the past. Your success is an act of war against the fear that has kept you small. Identify the biggest rules or expectations that have kept you trapped and break them. Do the thing you were told you should not or could not do and feel the rush of liberation.

5. **Lead with the energy of "I dare you to stop me."** At some point, you have to stop negotiating with yourself. You have to stop questioning if you are worthy. You have to stop playing small just because it makes others comfortable. Your new mindset should be, "I dare you to stop me." Say it to your fears. Say it to your doubts. Say it to anyone who tries to tell you that you cannot do something. Say it to *yourself*. When you start moving like you are inevitable, the Universe will adjust accordingly.

Most people stop in the "gap" because they mistake it for a dead end. It is not. It is a door. But it only opens when you walk toward it. The "gap" exists to see if you are ready. Are you? Or are you going to sit there and continue waiting for permission?

---

glow-up activation: the future you letter

Close your eyes and imagine yourself one year from now, after the breakthrough has occurred. The manifestation has arrived. You are living the life you have been working so hard to create. Visualize a full day in this future, where you wake up in the morning. What is surrounding you? How does it feel to be on the other side of the transformation, finally? Let the pride, peace, and joy of this version of you fully wash over your body.

When you feel connected to this vision, begin writing a letter from your future self to who you are today. Start with:

> Dear [Your Name], I am writing to you from the other side of the gap...

and let the words pour out. Let your future self thank you for not giving up, acknowledge the moments that felt heavy or confusing, and offer encouragement for the journey you are still on. When the letter is complete, fold it and place it in a sacred location. Revisit it any time doubt tries to creep in.

Record yourself reading it aloud in your most grounded and loving voice, if you'd like. Hearing it in your own words can be a transformative reminder that the gap is not a void but a bridge, and on the other side of that bridge is the life you have already claimed.

the seventh mystic key

The Manifesto

THE GRAND FINALE of all *The Mystic Keys* is the moment we bring it all together. And what better way to do that than with a manifesto? Now, before you start imagining some dramatic revolutionary speech or a scroll written in ancient calligraphy, I want to clear something up. A manifesto is a declaration. A statement of truth. A personal creed that says, "This is who I am, this is what I believe, and this is how I move through the world."

It sounds simple, right? But where most people trip up is that they do not think they are allowed to declare anything about themselves. Most people think that identity is something handed to them, something they have to accept. Your parents give you a name, and society gives you a job and a set of rules to follow. Before you realize that your personal autonomy has been sacrificed, you just nod along like obedient little Sims characters waiting for the next command.

But not now. Not anymore.

By now, you have solved the riddle. You have

reworked your thinking by shattering limiting beliefs and started sculpting a reality that actually serves you. But what good is all this internal transformation if you do not claim it? If you do not own it and say, "This is who I am now. This is what I stand for."

That is where your personal glow-up manifesto comes in.

A manifesto is not a wish list or a new vision board. It is not a prayer that you whisper into the void, hoping that some man in the clouds will grant you permission to be who you already are. A manifesto is a summoning of power through a decision. It is you deciding what will now be, and once you decide, your reality will bend accordingly to match it. In other words, reality does not move first. You do.

When you stand in your own truth, the Universe will listen. But if you second-guess your truth by writing your manifesto in pencil because you half-expect to erase and edit parts of it depending on other people's reactions, then you might as well crumple the whole thing up and start over, because a manifesto with disclaimers is not a manifesto. It is an apology, and you, my dear, are done apologizing for existing.

Now, what makes a manifesto work? Because a little birdie told me there are plenty of people out here writing down affirmations, taping them to their bathroom mirrors, and still wondering why their lives are not changing. This is because a real manifesto is not just words; it is an energetic shift that is governed by the energy that runs through your mind, your thoughts, and your belief systems.

When you write your manifesto, you are not just

stating facts; you are issuing commands to the fabric of existence. And this process requires more than just pretty sentences on your mirror. It requires real belief, which is why we did so much work on your thoughts and beliefs prior to this. It requires that you step fully into the person you are declaring your next-level version to be, but that means you have to see what your past version was.

When you set your manifesto, you are not just stating facts; you are initiating reality itself with your thoughts. You are issuing commands to the fabric of existence, and this process requires more than just pretty sentences on your mirror. It requires real belief, which is why we did so much work on your thoughts and beliefs prior to this. It requires that you step fully into the person you are declaring your next-level version to be, but that means you have to see what your past version was.

Your manifesto must be uncompromising and leave no room for negotiation. It should be so bold that you experience a twinge of nausea. If you feel comfortable with what goes into your manifesto, then you haven't gone far enough. We are bending reality here; it should make you a little nervous (in a good way).

And before your logical mind starts saying to yourself, "What if it is not true?" let me remind you that the truth is a construct. Every belief you hold and every limitation you have ever accepted were made up. You might as well make up something that serves you, because the thing that most people overlook is that life is already a manifesto. With every new day, with every self-deprecating thought, with every hesitant action, with every limited belief, you are writing a declaration about who you think you are.

Most people do not realize they already have a manifesto because it is not one they consciously created. It is the one given to them by parents, culture, religion, society, and all the unconscious agreements they never questioned. It is the manifesto that says, "Life is hard." "Success is for other people." "I am not good enough." "Money is evil." "Things never work out for me." Sound familiar? That is a default manifesto. It came with a fine print that you never read and never signed, but somehow agreed to live by. And like any bad contract, it keeps you bound until you consciously tear it up and write a new one.

Writing your glow-up manifesto is not just an intellectual exercise; it is an act of personal revolution, reclaiming who and what you already are but, up until this point, did not have the opportunity to fully express. It is also a magical act that sets reality in motion because words create. Have you ever noticed how spiritual texts say, "In the beginning was the Word?" Not "In the beginning was the brainstorming session," or "In the beginning was a strong vibe." No. The Word. This is why you cannot write your manifesto using words from your old belief systems.

I remember the exact moment I scrapped my old, raggedy-ass manifesto. It was one of those days when life was trying me. Have you ever had one of those? Where every little thing feels like an insult? My coffee was burnt, and I caught myself mid-thought, accepting struggle as a normal part of life. I paused. Wait a minute. When did I sign up for this? Whose rulebook was I following? Suddenly, the rules felt like trash.

So, I wrote a new one. But this time, it was not a list of goals or a hopeful wish. I wrote a law. A new declaration on how I was going to live my life. And when I was done, something inside me shifted. Not only did my energy change, but my decisions changed, and the way I moved changed too. Because the moment you put your truth in writing, you become bound to it. Not in a restrictive way, but in a divine contract with yourself kind of way.

A manifesto is a command. It is a reality-shaping decree. It is your law. Life does not have the power to say "no" to you. Life is not some divine HR department reviewing your application for success, deciding whether or not you are qualified for happiness. Life is a mirror, and it reflects what you declare. And this is exactly why affirmations do not work.

Now, before anyone gets offended, let me be clear. I am not saying affirmations are useless. They have their rightful place. But if we are going to be real, most people use them wrong. They stand in front of the mirror, looking unsure, and say, "I am wealthy. I am successful. I am confident." Meanwhile, their mind is screaming, "LIES! LIES! LIES!" Have you ever tried to lie to yourself? It does not work. Your subconscious is like, *Girl... we're still broke. Why are we lying?*

Affirmations are weak spells because they rely on hope instead of certainty. They are often just Band-Aids for your self-doubt. A manifesto, on the other hand, does not hope; it declares. It does not say, "I am confident." It says, "Confidence is my natural state. My voice carries weight. When I speak, people listen." Do you see the difference? One is wishful thinking, and the other is a law, a declaration. And that is the key.

The first thing you need to understand when writing your manifesto is that you are not negotiating. We do not negotiate with the terrorists of your mind. You are not asking the Universe if it is okay. You are not writing something you *hope* you will live by. You are writing something that *is*. The most powerful manifestos do not sound like they were written by someone trying to change their life. They sound like they were written by someone who already owns their life.

I remember the first time I wrote a weak manifesto. I was in my journal, trying to be all enlightened and stuff, and wrote something like, "I strive to live a life of purpose." "I hope to embody confidence." "I am working toward success." Do you see the problem? That sounds like someone asking for permission to be great. That sounds like someone hoping things change instead of declaring that they already have.

I caught myself, scratched all of that out, and wrote, "I move with purpose, and my presence is undeniable. Success is the natural result of who I am." See the difference?

A manifesto should sound like it is already true, because it is. Just because you cannot see yourself yet for who you really are does not mean your next-level version is not looking at you in the mirror. Conditioning prevents you from seeing, but you are still there. Your manifesto is not about who you *think* you are today. It's about who you've *decided* to be.

The reason a manifesto is so important is that reality

follows conviction. Have you ever noticed how some people just decide they are important, and the world agrees with them? They walk into a room with the energy of someone who expects to be listened to, and suddenly, people listen, even if they do not want to. That is because certainty bends reality.

Think about it. When you go to a restaurant, you do not sit there debating whether or not you deserve to eat. You do not look at the menu thinking, "I hope the waiter thinks I am worthy of the pasta." No. You open your mouth and say, "I will have the pasta." You decide. And when you decide, reality moves. The chef makes your food. The server brings it to you. No struggle, no hesitation. But when it comes to the bigger things like success, love, and abundance, people suddenly get weird. They start asking life instead of telling life. Your manifesto teaches you to tell.

Your Glow-Up Manifesto is your personal declaration of power, designed to finalize your new mindset and reshape your reality. Changing your thinking is great, but it doesn't mean much if you don't actively put it into motion. This is not just another journal entry full of weak affirmations; it is a command to the Universe that sets your new standard for life.

write with authority

Your manifesto is not a wish list. It is the law. Write in

the present tense, as if everything you declare is already true because it is!

- "I am magnetic. Opportunities flow to me effortlessly."
- Verdict: Truth
- "I hope to attract opportunities."
- Verdict: Trash

Use definitive language. No "try," "hope," or "maybe."

- "I command success in all I do."
- Verdict: Truth
- "I am trying to be more successful."
- Verdict: Trash

Be bold and unapologetic. Your manifesto should feel powerful when you read it.

identify your core beliefs

What do you stand for? Your glow-up manifesto is a reflection of your values, newfound mindset, and vision for your life. Ask yourself:

1. What are the non-negotiables in my life?
2. How do I expect to be treated by the world?
3. What do I believe about success, love, money, confidence, and self-worth?

Write these as statements of fact.

keep it short, commanding, and repeatable

Your manifesto is not an essay. It should be punchy, concise, and easy to remember because when you write an essay, you will try to justify your new truths and start over-explaining why things are now what they are. You said what you said.

1. Stick to 3-5 strong, impactful statements.
2. Each statement should be short, clear, and direct.
3. If you cannot repeat it from memory, it is too complicated. You are commanding, not over-explaining.

Example:

- "My decisions are final."
- "Reality adjusts to me."
- "My success is inevitable."

live by it—no exceptions

Your manifesto is the declaration of your new reality. That means every decision, action, and thought should align with it.

1. Ask yourself daily, "Am I acting in alignment with my manifesto?"
2. If you catch yourself doubting or acting out of alignment, course correct immediately.

3. Hold yourself accountable. No more playing small.

A manifesto is not just words on a piece of paper; it is the law of your life.

When you read your manifesto, does it feel like a law? Or does it feel like a *suggestion*? If it feels like a suggestion, start over and scratch out the weak language. Get rid of anything that sounds like *hope* or *maybe*. Rewrite it like you are speaking directly to reality and looking it in the face. Because once you write it, you are not just making a declaration to yourself; you are making a declaration to the Universe. And the Universe? It will listen to those who command to be heard.

---

glow-up activation: trashing the old manifesto

Most people try to add new beliefs on top of old ones, but that is weak magic. Instead, let's reverse-engineer your power by first identifying the default manifesto you have been living by. The one society, fear, and self-doubt wrote for you.

1. *Write down 3-5 false beliefs that you have lived by.*
    - *Be brutally honest. "I have to work twice as hard to get half of what they have." "Things*

never work out for me." "I cannot trust myself." "I have to play small to be accepted."
2. *Burn, Rip, or Trash It.*
   - *Destroy that nonsense. Rip up the paper, burn it (safely), or throw it away while saying, "I don't consent to this reality anymore."*

the glow-up

main character energy

TO EXPERIENCE the glow-up that brings you to your next level, you must believe the world revolves around you. Now, does it really? It depends on who or what you ask. From the perspective of your friends, family, and even colleagues, I suspect they will claim that the world does not, in fact, revolve around you. But from the perspective of the Universe, you are the only thing it sees. Why? Because you were created by the thing that makes all things, therefore making you an aspect of that all-powerful thing itself.

Society will have you convinced that you are not important and will shove you into a corner as if you are disposable for being too many things or not enough. Too loud, too fat, too short, too tall. Not funny enough. Not smart enough. And yada yada. It will fill your mind to the brim with falsehoods. Then, when you start to sense your magic and get a glimpse of the light you have been concealing, before you turn it all the way back on, you will first question whether it is safe to do so.

But that next-level life you want is meant for the person who knows they not only deserve to have it but are also willing to take it. It is the version of you who recognizes that naysayers have no place in your new world. It is the version of you who has realized that you can write your own story and that all good stories have a main character. And because this is your story, that main character is you.

When you fully embody main character energy, you are stepping into the truth of your existence. You are reclaiming your place as the center of your own Universe. Not to be narcissistic. Not to be self-absorbed. But because *someone* has to be at the center, and if not you, then who? If you are not the lead, you are relegating yourself to a side role in a life that was handcrafted for you. What is the point of living a life designed for you but still playing an extra when you are supposed to be the lead actor?

The reason most people struggle with their confidence, self-worth, and manifesting their desires is that they are miscast in their own lives. They are auditioning for a role that is already theirs and then waiting for permission to walk into a spotlight that was designed specifically for them. But main character energy is not something you wait to be given. It is something you *decide* to claim by simply walking into your own spotlight and accepting your glow-up.

When you deny yourself the role of the main character, you give away your power because you open the door for other people to claim the things that belong to you. You dim your light. You shrink in conversations.

You suppress your desires. And after all of that, you convince yourself that being "humble," "realistic," or "considerate" means staying small. Then, over time, you begin to feel invisible in your own life and start blaming cosmic forces. But here is the gag: the world did not make you invisible. *You chose not to be seen.*

This shows up in every aspect of your life. You say yes when you mean no. You apologize for things you did not do. You downplay your accomplishments. You settle for crumbs and then try to convince yourself you are full. But we both know you are not. You are starving for recognition, freedom, and to be seen, heard, and celebrated as you truly are. And most importantly, starving for the opportunity to remove all the masks of things you are not.

You were born to thrive and shine, and the longer you resist that truth, the more life will feel off and misaligned. Because when you reject your own main character status, life becomes a series of scenes where you never get the spotlight, never get the mic, and never get the climax. You will just fade into the background.

So, what happens when you truly accept that you are the main character?

Your energy will shift as your aura changes. You will start walking and talking differently and taking up space without feeling obligated to apologize for it. And people feel it. Suddenly, your presence will start commanding attention in the spaces you want to be seen in, without needing to use a whole lot of effort.

Moving with your main character energy activates a

frequency. We live in a vibrational Universe where people sense and feel before they understand. People feel your energy before they know your name and before they hear your words, making them feel like they knew what you were going to say before you said it. This is why some people know when their boss is walking down the hallway toward their office.

So, if you are walking around with "supporting character" energy, life will treat you accordingly. You will find yourself being overlooked for promotions or being passed over in conversations, even though you are actively trying to make a point.

But when you shift your internal frequency, when you decide to be the star of your own show, everything around you adjusts. Opportunities appear. People pay attention. Doors open. Not because you are suddenly more "deserving," but because you finally matched the energy of the version of you who already has it.

Desire alone does not manifest results. But moving like it does. You can want the glow-up all day long, but if you do not *become* the version of yourself who receives it, the Universe has nothing to respond to. Main character energy is the vibration that signals to the Universe, "It is mine now, thank you." When you *think* like the main character, your entire energy field shifts, and reality has no choice but to follow suit and shift with it.

We often associate main character energy with big moments or mile markers that include spotlights, accolades, or viral attention, but some of the most powerful examples of your main character energy happened in quiet, everyday scenes, and because they did not feel loud or dramatic, you overlooked them. But make no mistake: you were the star. The energy was real, and you were transforming in real time. You just did not realize it yet.

Remember when you walked away from a relationship, job, or situation even though everyone around you thought you were crazy? They said, "You are making a mistake." "You are being too emotional." "Are you sure?" And at that time, you probably did not have a neat explanation or the ability to articulate all the reasons. All you knew was that something inside you said, "No. I am done."

That was main character energy. Choosing yourself without needing a vote from a committee. That was the moment you stopped letting others write your story and took the pen back into your hands.

Maybe it was that time when you decided to go back to school, start a side hustle, move to a new city, or apply for something you "were not qualified for." You told yourself it was just a test run, just an idea, but deep down, it was you stepping into a bigger version of yourself. The next-level version.

The main characters have big dreams. They always want more, and at that moment, you did, too. You were not being unrealistic; you were being expansive.

Think back to your lowest moment. Was it the heartbreak that wrecked you? The loss that gutted you? Or was it the failure that made you question everything you thought you knew to be true? You thought you would not get through it, but somehow, you did. You cried about it. Raged a bit. Maybe doubted a little. But you still kept showing up. Day by day, you picked up the pieces, and when you emerged on the other side, you were not the same person. You were wiser, stronger, and bolder.

That is what the main characters do. They fall apart, get up again, and transform. The pain is not pointless. It is part of the plot. Have you ever had a moment when you entered a space, and people felt you before you even said a word? You walked in, and eyes turned? That was you shifting the energy of the room. People may not have said anything out loud, but the room acknowledged you. Only a main character could do that.

There was a time when you were so used to people-pleasing. You over-gave without receiving anything in return. You over-explained something because someone kept questioning you, even though you were the expert on the subject. But then, one day, something clicked, and you said no, knowing that you did not want to look back.

Perhaps you ended a friendship, blocked a number, canceled plans, or stopped answering calls that were draining you. That was the moment you realized that protecting your peace is the plotline. That was main character boundary-setting. And then, subtly, this main character energy triggered glowing moments in your life. Perhaps you couldn't see it at that time. But here and there, things lit up.

It might have happened on a dance floor, while

working on a creative project, in a conversation with your best friend, or while watching a silly video. In that moment, you felt alive. Pure joy poured out of you effortlessly. You lost track of time and were not trying to impress anyone. You were just *in it*, being yourself. That was your glow. People probably told you afterward, "There is something about you." "You are glowing." "I do not know what it is, but I love your energy." They were witnessing your light because you were already living it.

But now, it is time to move like it until one day, everything shifts. You do the thing they did not see coming. You get the job. You launch the brand. You leave the situation. You speak up, step out, or level up in a way that makes people pause and ask you, "Wait… when did you become like this?" They did not realize you were evolving the whole time. But you knew it all along, and that is the only thing that counts. And that is the thing about main characters; they do not need to announce the plot twist. They are the plot twist.

You already are the main character. You just need to remember and connect the dots between all the moments you brushed off, downplayed, or forgot. Because the person who made the hard decision, left the toxic relationship, started from scratch, rose after failure, or dared to dream bigger? They were not a side character. They were you.

This is about recognizing and calling your power back from every chapter where you doubted yourself, and from every scene where you allowed yourself to fade into the background of your own story.

There will be no more accidental glow-ups and no more waiting for the stars to align or someone else to validate your spotlight. You will now do this on purpose. Living in your main character era intentionally means showing up deliberately. Here is how to do exactly that:

be the main character daily

This is about identity. You need to know who you are choosing to be. What is your new next-level vibe? What do you believe now? What do you no longer tolerate? What is your calling? This will determine your behavior, which in turn determines your results. So start here:

1. Write a character bio for your main character self. Describe yourself like a screenwriter developing a lead role: your energy, your habits, your routines, your look, your inner world.
2. Every morning, ask yourself, "What would the main character version of me do today?" Then do that.

romanticize the hell out of your life

Your life is not a documentary. You are the full-blown cinematic experience, and you get to direct it. Romanticizing your life does not mean ignoring reality; it means infusing your reality with meaning and significance. Make ordinary moments feel sacred. Try this:

1. Play music while doing mundane tasks. This can make sipping a cup of coffee a ritual or a walk in the park look like a montage.
2. Have some fun by occasionally dressing as if someone is always filming you, because, energetically, you are always being seen.
3. Make even the hard days feel poetic. Document the rich arc in your journal by capturing all of the tension, heartbreak, and contrast. The story is still yours to write.

stop explaining yourself to other people

The main characters do not over-explain. They make bold moves, and the world adjusts to the new reality. You do not need to give a 10-slide PowerPoint presentation to justify your glow-up, newfound boundaries, the shifts in your behavior, or your decision to walk away. You do not owe an explanation for your transformation. Say less and move more. From now on, let these words be your motto: "Because I said so."

make your environment reflect your era

The energy around you should match the energy *within you*. If your space feels outdated, cluttered, or uninspiring, it's time for a set redesign.

1. Clean up your physical space and get rid of what no longer fits your next-level self.
2. Clean out your digital space by unfollowing people who drain you.

3. Use scent, lighting, colors, and visuals in your living space that activate your creativity and make you feel inspired.
4. Create a "main character" playlist that instantly shifts your mood and reminds you of who the hell you are.

Your environment will either reinforce your personal power or erode it. Be intentional with everything that you do as your next-level self.

build a ritual of self-devotion

This means learning how to make room for yourself after spending all your years making room for other people when they neglected to make room for you. It means making time daily to pour into yourself and, through the continuation of this practice, cultivating your inner reverence. This is deeper than self-care and self-love. This is about spiritual maintenance and nurturing your energetic hygiene. Try this:

1. Start your morning with intention setting.
2. Journal like you are writing your autobiography in real-time, because you are. If someone were to find it after your time on Earth has ended, what would you want them to read?
3. Talk to yourself in the mirror as if you're hyping up your best friend.
4. Celebrate small wins because they deserve some love, too.

Self-devotion is about reminding your nervous system, *I got me. I am the one I have been waiting for.*

create your own plotlines

Waiting around for something exciting to happen is supporting character energy. Main characters do not wait; they initiate. Life does not hand you excitement. You have to create it. Start spicing up your life by giving yourself chapters, arcs, and character development. Your life gets richer the moment you start writing your own scenes.

1. Assign each month a theme or title, such as *Soft Girl Spring* or *The Healing Era*.
2. Create mini-missions and complete them. Go on solo dates, try new things, or learn new skills.
3. Join a new meetup group to make some friends.

let people adjust or exit

When you start living as the main character, some people will not like it. They were used to your supporting role in their life, and now they have to recast. They were comfortable with the version of you who dimmed, paused, and tiptoed around their comfort.

Let them be uncomfortable.

Main characters do not negotiate their spotlight to

appease the extras. Your glow will activate some and repel others, but that is not your business.

You were never meant to play small in your own story and were always meant to be the main character. Reclaiming your role as the main character is the energetic shift needed to move you to the next level. You had moments where you were already living as the lead, but didn't realize it. You did that by choosing yourself, setting boundaries, and walking away from things that no longer serve you. And by doing that, you made decisions that aligned with your higher self, even when they did not make sense to anyone else. Those were not coincidences; they were evidence that your main character energy was already active. But now, you are going to do it on purpose by shifting from accidental glow-ups to an intentional one, because the spotlight has always been yours. You just have to stand in it.

---

glow-up activation: the main character audition

Stand in front of a mirror and imagine you are auditioning for the role of the main character in a movie about your life. How would you portray yourself? What emotions would you convey? What posture would you adopt? Use body language, tone, and facial expressions to embody the energy of the main character.

Record a 30-second video where you embody the main character of your life, speaking directly to the camera as if you were addressing your audience or future self. Play it back and notice what feelings or insights arise when you see yourself acting in this empowered way.

dream bigger, babe
Your Vision Board Needs an Upgrade

IF YOU WANT A BIGGER, more next-level life, you must think bigger, more next-level thoughts. The majority of the thoughts you routinely have are small and unproductive. It is not that your current thoughts are meaningless; it is that there is no awareness or intention behind the majority of your current thoughts. Because deliberate intention has not been used to think what you think, your thoughts have defaulted into various belief systems that keep you small and hidden.

Most people do not realize they are thinking small because "small" is the default setting. It is the mental autopilot that kicks in when you are not intentionally choosing something greater. Small thoughts are sneaky because they sound reasonable and responsible. They even sound like self-protection. But do not be fooled. Small thoughts are dream killers dressed in practicality, and your future is too big to keep playing these tiny mind games with yourself.

A "small thought" is any thought that shrinks your possibility, minimizes your power, or limits what you believe is available to you. A small thought is what you think when you're trying to avoid disappointment rather than activating potential. It is rooted in fear, not vision, and it is usually packaged in the kind of logic that seems smart but keeps you stuck. If your thoughts are small, your life will shrink to match them.

Thinking small has been the baseline for so long, it feels normal and familiar. Comfortable, even. However, small thinking does not manifest as you sitting in a corner whispering, "I do not believe in myself." It is more subtle than that. It sounds like, "Maybe next year." It sounds like, "Let me just wait until things calm down." It sounds like, "That would be nice, but it is not realistic."

Small thinking is so embedded in the culture that we have started calling it wisdom. We praise it for being practical, grounded, and responsible. But if you listen closely, you will notice that these so-called "wise" thoughts are often soaked in fear. They come from a deep place of uncertainty and hesitation to dream too big, because dreaming too big risks disappointment, failure, and being seen but not chosen. But thinking small does not protect you from pain; it just ensures you will never feel the thrill of expansion.

Vision boards are fun because this is where people claim the life of their dreams: six figures, freedom, love, luxury. Then they immediately follow it with thoughts that contradict that very vision. They will declare themselves ready to be a successful content creator, then turn around and second-guess every post they make, wondering if they should delete it because it didn't receive enough likes. They will say things like they want to write a bestselling book, but when it comes time to sit down and write, they start spiraling into self-doubt, stuck on one sentence because they have already convinced themselves no one will read it.

This is what I mean when I say your vision board needs an upgrade. The images you cut out and paste are big, but the thoughts you think are small. The frequency does not match. You cannot put a luxury villa on your board and then spend all day thinking, "I do not know if I can afford groceries next week." You cannot manifest the love of your life while constantly thinking, "Everyone always leaves me."

And I am not saying you have to fake it. I'm saying you need to upgrade your baseline. Your thoughts are setting the ceiling for your life, and most of you are living in rooms with six-foot ceilings, while that villa on your board has floor-to-ceiling windows. Every time you think a thought that is rooted in fear, doubt, or lack, you are reinforcing the very reality you are trying to break free from.

Now, I will give you the benefit of the doubt because the tricky part is that most small thoughts do not announce themselves or scream, "Hey! I am self-sabotage!" They come dressed as humility, or logic, or someone else's voice you internalized when you were too young to know better. They feel like your voice now, which makes them much harder to catch. That is why awareness is the first Mystic Key—because you cannot change a thought you don't even realize you are thinking.

I used to think small all the time without realizing it. I thought I was being realistic when I made backup plans for my dreams while simultaneously convincing myself that I should always have a Plan B, when I could have just committed to Plan A. I thought I was being humble when I downplayed my gifts so that other people wouldn't feel uncomfortable around me. I thought I was being wise when I avoided taking risks, as I didn't want to "waste time." But what I was really doing was living life on a delay and then getting mad at time for taking too long to produce that one dream on the vision board. I was regularly pushing pause on my potential while waiting for permission that was never going to come.

Small thoughts feel safe because they require nothing from you. No stretch. No leap. No courage. But they also offer you nothing. They are empty calories for your mind. You can spend your entire life thinking thoughts like, "Let me just get my ducks in a row," or "I will start when I feel more confident," and never realize that you have just spent ten years waiting for a moment that only arrives when you go first.

Small thoughts are everywhere. In the quiet moments, in your morning routine, in how you talk to yourself when no one is listening. They sneak in when you are brushing your teeth, scrolling on your phone, or deciding what to wear. They show up as that familiar little voice that tries to keep you in your lane.

You wake up in the morning and feel a burst of inspiration because maybe today is the day you finally start that blog, apply for that grant, or pitch that idea. But just as quickly as the spark arrives, here comes the small thought, tiptoeing in like, "But who is going to read it?" or "There are already so many people doing this." And just like that, the idea that could have changed your life gets filed away under "maybe later."

You see a job posting for a role that excites you. It's something that can elevate your income, influence, and your whole next-level life. You start reading through it and feel your pulse quicken. But then you catch a line at the bottom that says, "five years of experience," and suddenly, your brain says, "You are not qualified. Do not embarrass yourself." Those are small thoughts. They do not care about your potential. They just want to protect your ego from rejection.

Or maybe you are in a conversation with someone who intimidates you a little. You have something brilliant to say, a perspective that could shift the whole dialogue, but instead, you bite your tongue. You think, "They probably already know that," or "I do not want to sound stupid." Once again, a small thought. But this one is robbing you of your voice.

Small thoughts can dominate even in something as simple as choosing what to wear. You pick the safer outfit, the neutral colors, because your mind tells you, "That is too loud for work," or "People will think I am trying too hard." And your small thoughts win by convincing you to dim your light to keep others comfortable.

And do not even get me started on money. You see something you love and want, like a course, a trip, or a piece of art. But instead of asking, "How can I afford this?" your first thought is, "I cannot afford that." That is a shutdown thought. A small thought that ends a dream. There is no possibility because it blocks it.

Small thoughts are so casual that they sound like facts. "That is just how it is." "That is not in the cards for me." "I have missed my window." But none of that is true; it is programming. It is a habit that makes survival-mode thinking pretend to be realism.

You have to be bold enough to think beyond your current life—not just dream it, but think it. Make it normal in your mind. This requires stretching your mind beyond what you have glued to your vision board. Your life cannot grow bigger than your dominant thoughts. And if you are not deliberate, your dominant thoughts are probably the same recycled limitations you have been thinking about for years.

So, when I say your vision board needs an upgrade, I am not just talking about the images. I am talking about the frequency you are tuned to when you look at it. If you are staring at a board full of yachts, first-class flights, and your bestselling book cover, but your thoughts are stuck in "How will I ever afford that," then we have got work to do. The vision board is not magic. *You are*. And until your thoughts rise to meet the level of your desires, the vision board will just be wallpaper.

Expanding your thinking means stretching the boundaries of your internal world so they match the scale of the life you want to create. Your outer reality is always reflecting your inner landscape and mirrors your thoughts, belief systems, and expectations. If your current life feels limited, it is not because the world is holding you back. It is because your thinking has not yet stretched wide enough to allow more in.

Small thoughts keep you in energetic contraction. They create mental loops, making you go round and round your hesitation by second-guessing every idea you have ever had. These thoughts are not necessarily wrong, as they have probably served you well at one point. But today, they are outdated. They were formed at a time when playing small kept you safe, unnoticed, or in control. But those same thoughts become cages when you are trying to grow.

Expansive thinking is about deliberately interrupting habitual thoughts and replacing them with thoughts that align with possibility. These are bigger, bolder thoughts that pull you forward, rather than keeping you where you are. This is not about wishful thinking or blind optimism. It is about thinking with intention and thinking from vision instead of circumstance. You want to train your mind to lead instead of doing what it has always done, which is following.

Most people try to change their lives by changing their circumstances. They may get a new job, move to a new city, or try to find a new partner. But those things will not stick unless your thinking evolves with them. Because when you attempt to take your small thoughts into a bigger life, you will find a way to shrink that life right back down to what feels familiar. You will self-sabotage or play it safe because your inner world has not caught up to your new, next-level vision.

To expand your thinking, you must create new

patterns of thought that become stronger the more you choose them. And like any muscle, this requires repetition. Your mind is a brilliant machine, but it prioritizes what is familiar, so if you have been rehearsing small thoughts for a lifetime, then your brain will default to them unless you train it to do otherwise.

This is more than just a mindset shift. It is a mental reconditioning. You are not just thinking differently for a day or two. You are teaching your mind how to speak a new language, the language of your vision board and your next level.

So, how do you do it?

catch the small thought in real time

Transforming your thoughts into gold requires awareness, and so does expansion. You cannot change what you do not notice. Begin observing your thoughts as if you were a witness. When you hear yourself thinking things like, "I am not ready," "That is too much," or "I could never do that," pause. That is a small thought. Do not judge it; just catch it. That is the first breakthrough.

ask better questions

Instead of shutting things down with "I cannot do this" or "I do not know how," ask, "What would this look like if it were possible?" "What would I think if I fully believed in myself?" "What is the version of this thought that feels one size bigger?" A good question can function like an opportunity because it guides your brain toward new possibilities.

remember the vision, not the circumstance

Most people think from the perspective of their bank account, their current job, or their past failures. Think from the perspective of the version of you who already has what you want. Let your thoughts reflect where you are going, not where you have been. What would you think about this moment if you had the life, confidence, love, and success you dream of? Think that thought now.

replace it, do not reject it

It is not enough to stop a small thought. You must give your mind a new thought to hold on to, or it will start to grasp for something. Instead of "That is too expensive," replace it with "I am expanding into the version of me who can afford this with ease." Instead of "I am not good enough," try "I am learning to see myself clearly. My value is not up for debate." This is not about lying to yourself; it is about upgrading your next-level thought, and you do that in steps by replacing a small thought with a slightly bigger one.

mental dress rehearsal

Your brain does not know the difference between a real experience and a vividly imagined one. You can be as creative as you can, and if you say it is true, your mind will agree with you. Use this to your advantage. Spend five minutes a day thinking *from* your expanded life.

Feel it. Walk through a future day in your mind. The more real it feels, the more familiar it becomes. And the more familiar it becomes, the less resistance you will have to living it.

move like the bigger thought

Do not wait for the thought to feel true because you may be waiting for eternity. Act on it. Expand your thinking into behavior. Don't just think about a new job; apply for the job. Don't just think about raising your prices; raise your prices. Don't just think about booking a trip; book the trip. And say no to all the things that do not match your bigger thought. Every action you take from a bigger thought reinforces it and creates a new baseline for what your mind finds familiar.

Expanding your thinking is not a one-time event. It is a daily decision and a constant choice that is made. It is a refusal to let the mind shrink your potential and close doors in the face of your possibilities. The more you do it, the easier it becomes. The thoughts that used to scare you will eventually feel normal. And then you will have the opportunity to expand again by implementing even bigger thoughts.

So next time your mind tries to play small, stop and ask, "Is this thought worthy of the next-level life I am creating?" If not, upgrade it.

And choose big. Always. The worst-case scenario is that you will get what you asked for.

glow-up activation: 10x the vision

Write out your goals, dreams, career ambitions, personal desires, and where you want to be in the next one to five years. It can be things like, "I want to grow my business by 30% next year," "I want to travel to Europe once this year," or "I want to get promoted to Senior Manager by next year."

Now, look at what you have written and ask yourself, "What feels small, and what could be done without much effort?" Challenge yourself to recognize where you have limited yourself and played it safe.

Look at each item you just wrote down and multiply it by 10. I am not talking about just adding a little more. I am talking about blowing it way out of proportion. Push the boundaries of what you think is possible. If you had, "I want to get promoted to Senior Manager," rewrite it as, "I want to be offered a VP position within the next year and lead a high-impact team in a global company."

Close your eyes and imagine that your 10x vision is already real. You have already achieved everything you just wrote down, and you are now living in your future. How do you feel? What do you see around you? What do you hear?

Now, let us upgrade that vision board. Grab magazines or printouts and create your "10x the Vision" vision board. This vision board will reflect the new, massive life you have just shifted into.

call in your soulmate

Heart Rehab for the Heartbroken

IF I HAD a dollar for every time a client asked me to help them clean up their love life, I would be rich enough not to have to write this book. But there is something that revealed itself in all of those experiences that I have always found fascinating, and that is that love is the number one interest people have. Whether that is finding love, keeping love, recovering from a lost love, or making love, people would do anything to figure out how to manage it in their own lives.

The caveat is that people spend more time trying to manage it, rather than allowing themselves to heal from the initial mismanagement of it, and as a result, they end up operating from a place of wounding rather than from a place of empowerment. Love ends up feeling painful, as opposed to feeling like it should feel, which is expansive, inviting, and inspirational.

I suspect that many of you have added love to your manifesto, and for those of you who haven't, a little heart rehab would still do you some good.

To access this thing we call love, you must undergo

your own heart rehab. Why? To clean yourself up enough that you stop self-sabotaging, ruining your chances, and picking the wrong partners. In order to experience love, you have to take accountability for the role you play in it.

Let's talk about the part that most people skip over when they're calling in their soulmate: themselves. You have been taught to focus on the other person. What they did or what they did not do. The fact that they ghosted you. The fact that they cheated on you. The fact that they did not love you the way you needed them to. You replay their actions, over-analyze their words, and then build entire psychological profiles around their behavior that you share in a group chat with your friends. But have you ever sat down and asked yourself why you let them stay? Did you ever ask yourself why you tolerated their inconsistency? Why did you ignore the red flags that were waving like carnival banners?

This is not about blaming yourself, because maybe, at that time, you did not know better. This is about establishing awareness (the first Mystic Key).

Your current love life is the result of your current belief system. Period.

You can say you want a soulmate and can write it down in your manifestation journal. You can even visualize them bringing you flowers every Sunday and cuddling you as you heal your inner child. But if your limiting beliefs are telling you that love is dangerous, unreliable, disappointing, or something you have to earn, then your manifestations will not stick, because what you actually believe will override what you say you want. Here are some common limited beliefs regarding love:

love equals pain

So many people walk around with the belief that love hurts. Not just heartbreak but love itself. You may have witnessed or experienced dysfunctional love growing up that was chaotic, unpredictable, abusive, or conditional. Somewhere deep inside, you linked love with anxiety, hypervigilance, and performing for approval. As an adult, you find yourself chasing partners who replicate that experience and partners who make you question your worth, keep you guessing, or withhold affection as a form of control.

If this is you, then your nervous system has mistaken *wounding* for *chemistry*. It is not that you are unlucky in love. It is that your system is addicted to what is familiar. And what is familiar is not love; it is fear.

love has to be earned

If you find yourself bending over backward, shape-shifting in order to fit into your beloved's ideal type, and being the "perfect partner" just to keep someone around, chances are this belief is running the show. Somewhere along the line, you internalized the idea that love is a reward for good behavior. You learned that someone would finally choose you if you did enough, gave enough, or proved yourself.

So you overgive.

You overfunction, which attracts people who are more than happy to take from you but never truly show up *for* you. And when they leave, you tell yourself you were not enough. However, the truth is that you were doing too much. Love that is real does not require a performance. It does not require a sacrifice of self. It meets you where you are, and it loves you for who you are, not what you do.

i don't deserve *healthy* love

This one is sneaky. On the surface, you will say you want a healthy relationship. You will make vision boards with couple goals and pin weddings on Pinterest. But when someone actually comes along who is kind, consistent, emotionally available, and genuinely interested in you, what happens? You run and sometimes even hide. You friend-zone them and say they are boring. Next thing you know, you're saying there's no spark. Why? Because healthy love feels unfamiliar. It feels unsafe and too calm. You are used to chaos, to the high of the chase, to the rollercoaster of "Will they text me back?"

Healthy love does not offer that adrenaline. It offers peace and serenity. And if you are not used to peace, you will mistake it for a lack of passion.

it's too late for me

If you have experienced heartbreak after heartbreak, it's easy to believe that real love is just not in the cards for you. You might say things like, "All the good ones are taken," "Dating is trash these days," or "I attract nothing but emotionally avoidant people." However, the fact is that those are not just observations you have made. They are *agreements* you have made with your pain. And as long as you hold onto those agreements, they become self-fulfilling prophecies and the basis of your belief system.

When you believe love has passed you by, you energetically remove yourself from the game. You stop showing up fully and sabotage new opportunities before they even begin. And then you start settling for crumbs because you have convinced yourself that's all you're going to get. But love is not age-restricted. It is not something you "miss out" on. It is something you align with, and alignment begins with belief.

What do you believe about love? Not what you hope. Not what you post on Instagram. What do you actually believe in your quiet moments when you are by yourself and no one else is listening? Do you believe love is safe? Do you believe love is for you? Do you believe love is already on its way? Or do you believe you have to struggle, suffer, and settle just to feel a fraction of it? Because whatever you believe, you will prove yourself right.

This is where we start the rehab process. We are not going to do it by jumping into another situationship or re-downloading the dating app. We are going to do it by becoming the next-level version of you who no longer entertains relationships that betray your values.

This version of you is clear and calm. This version of you is no longer trying to earn someone's affection or convince someone to see your worth. They have already chosen themselves, and from that energy, they naturally attract love that feels like truth instead of an item on a wish list.

Your love life does not change when someone new shows up. It changes when you show up differently and when you stop waiting to be chosen and realize that you are the one doing the choosing.

You are the writer, the casting director, the star, and the narrator of your own love story. And you do not need to wait for permission to give your heart a happy ending. You just need to stop living in the heartbreak plot.

Now that you have identified the love beliefs holding you hostage, it is time to challenge them (the second Mystic Key).

Beliefs are not facts. A belief is just a repeated thought that has gained enough momentum to become your default thought. It is not *the* truth. It is *your* truth, which means it can be rewritten.

Let us take one of the most common love beliefs: "All the good ones are taken." Challenge it. Is that *really* true? Or is it trash? Has your brain simply tuned into relationships that support that belief? Have you ever met someone in a happy, healthy relationship and thought, "Where did they find a person like that?" Exactly. They exist.

They are out here, but your brain, operating under the old belief system, does not register them as available. You scroll past them. You write them off as "not your type." You self-select out of those connections without realizing it. Your beliefs determine what you perceive as possible, so if your belief is that love is scarce, hard, or painful, you will find constant evidence to support it. You are not cursed. You are just programmed.

That is why challenging the belief is so important. You are poking holes in the illusion you have been living inside. Here is how to do it for love:

look for counter-evidence

Find real-life examples that contradict your belief. You know or have heard of at least one person who found love later in life, or one person who left a toxic relationship and found someone who adored them. Or that one person who did not follow the rules and still ended up wildly loved. That is proof that your belief is not universal. It is just *yours*.

ask who taught you that belief

Was it your parents? A heartbreak? A culture (or an app, perhaps?) that profits off your insecurity? Most of your beliefs about love were not chosen; they were inherited, and inherited beliefs are rarely aligned with your personal truth.

ask what your belief protects you from

Every limiting belief serves a purpose. "Love never lasts" might protect you from vulnerability, while "I always get hurt" might protect you from intimacy. Your belief is not just holding you back; it is also helping you avoid something you fear. The trick is identifying that fear.

When you start dismantling your love beliefs, you will feel uncomfortable, but that's a good thing. It means you are shifting to your next-level version.

Your ego will resist it. Your body might tighten up. You may even want to retreat to the safety of the familiar (do not text them back!). But I need you to keep going. Because what is on the other side of that resistance is not just a better relationship; it is emotional freedom. You are not here to repeat your past. You are here to transcend it.

Now that you have cracked open the old story, it is time to reframe your thoughts (the third Mystic Key).

This is where you reclaim your narrative. Remember that reframing is the art of shifting how you view something so that it empowers you, rather than diminishing you. The facts do not change, but your relationship to the facts does. Let us revisit a few of those common love beliefs and give them a glow-up:

- **Old Belief:** Love hurts.

- **Reframe:** Real love heals. What hurt was my attachment to people who were not equipped to love me in a healthy way. I am no longer available for pain disguised as passion.

- **Old Belief:** I always get abandoned.
- **Reframe:** I now recognize that I used to choose people who mirrored my own fear of intimacy. I no longer abandon myself, and that means I no longer attract people who do so, either.

- **Old Belief:** I am not enough to be truly loved.
- **Reframe:** I am deeply lovable, exactly as I am. I do not have to perform, earn, or prove anything to anybody. The right person will love me with ease, not conditions.

- **Old Belief:** I am always too much.
- **Reframe:** I am the perfect amount for the right person. My passion, my power, and my presence are gifts, not problems. I no longer dim my light to make those who refuse to shine comfortable.

- **Old Belief:** I do not trust love.
- **Reframe:** I trust myself to navigate love with my wisdom and newfound clarity. Love is not something to fear; it is something to discern. I am now equipped to choose my partners with intention.

See the shift? When you reframe your beliefs around love, you are not pretending your pain did not happen. You are transforming the meaning of that pain and saying, "Yes, that happened, but it no longer defines me." You are no longer a victim of your romantic history.

This is how you glow up your love life—not by finding the perfect person, but by becoming the person who is a match for the love you desire. When your beliefs shift, your standards shift, and your choices shift too. When your choices shift, your entire love life undergoes a transformation.

You will begin to feel different in your body when someone does not meet your standard, and you stop chasing, questioning yourself, or collapsing your boundaries. You simply say, "This is not aligned with my next-level version," and keep it moving. That is what it means to move from wounded love to empowered love.

Let us be real. Most people have been walking through the world asking, "How can I get someone to love me?" But your new question is, "How can I love myself enough only to entertain what aligns with that love?" Because when you choose yourself and upgrade your inner dialogue, you shift the beliefs that used to keep you in patterns of lack, triggering a glow-up that becomes magnetic and noticeable to others. Suddenly, the same people who did not value you will circle back, confused. Not because they have changed, but because your frequency has changed. And now, you will be able to see them clearly. They were never your person. They were just part of your pattern.

You do not just hope for love. You become the version of you who already has it. This is where most people get stuck because they rewrite the story but keep showing up as the same character. They write the new script but keep rehearsing the old lines.

You are not doing that anymore. You are shifting the vibe entirely.

You must embody your new love life (the fifth Mystic Key) by walking through the world as someone who knows love is not a question, because it's a natural part of life. You do not chase, beg, prove, or plead with old or new partners. You sit back, centered in your own self-worth, knowing that what aligns with your energy will find you and stay with you.

You trust your "yes." You trust your "no." You stop explaining your standards to people who do not deserve explanations, and you stop negotiating your needs with people who are not equipped to meet them.

You shift from scarcity to sufficiency. From "I hope they like me" to "I hope they align." From "Why do they not want me?" to "Do I want them?"

This is the moment you stop abandoning yourself for the illusion of connection. It is about holding your position (the sixth Mystic Key), not shrinking, wavering, or contorting yourself to fit into someone else's storyline. You become the one people rise to meet.

And yes, you will be tempted as your old patterns—or your ex—try to seduce you. They will show up in a prettier package, with slightly better manners, but they will still feel like anxiety, confusion, and inconsistency in your body.

This is because you are now moving like someone

who is already loved, because you are. And when you move like it, the world mirrors it. Love responds to you, and relationships shift to match your new frequency.

You will no longer need to convince anyone of your worth, because people will sense the change within you. They will either meet you or fall away. But regardless of which way, that is not your concern. You are no longer adjusting your crown for people who were never meant to sit beside you on the throne.

Here is what your new love manifesto should sound like:

> I AM love. I am worthy of love that expands me, not contracts me. I no longer chase affection, and I radiate self-worth, letting love meet me at my next level. My heart is clear, my standards are non-negotiable, and my presence is magnetic. I trust that the love meant for me will feel peaceful, safe, and aligned. I will never again choose confusion and call it passion. I am fully embodied, and love is already mine.

The glow-up does not mean perfection; it means choosing differently. It was never about getting someone else to love you. It was about you loving yourself so deeply that anyone who does not match that energy becomes irrelevant.

So, if your heart is still tender, be gentle, but be firm.

This is your heart rehab. This is the opportunity to stop making love a battlefield and start making it a sanctuary for you. And from this healed, whole, radiant place, you don't find your soulmate; you will *recognize* them.

glow-up activation: heart rehab

Place your hands on your heart. Breathe deeply and visualize your heart expanding with warmth, compassion, and unconditional love. Imagine this energy radiating outward, filling the space around you. As you do this, mentally send love to your past relationships, forgiving them for the lessons they taught you.

Afterward, write a letter to your future soulmate, new best friend, or a family member you would like to move forward with. Describe the love you are ready to give and receive. What do you need to let go of to make space for this relationship? Bury the letter in the earth or burn it, symbolizing your release and your readiness for a new chapter in love.

transform your money mindset

NOW, what good is a glow-up if it does not come with some abundance? If we are going to be honest with each other, most people think of glow-ups as coming with a side of more money and resources. Perhaps a BMW? A nice pair of Gucci sunglasses? Maybe it was a trip to the spa for a one-hour massage instead of a 30-minute one.

I personally find money blocks the most interesting because it is the one thing that people view as outside of themselves and, therefore, outside of their command. Because we physically hold money, we interpret it to be separate from us, and it is through this other-ism that people find excuses and reasoning for why they can never have a piece of the pie.

If you are going to bust through this block, you must first understand that struggle is a mindset. It is part of your thought patterns and, to be frank, an outdated, limited belief that you have been carrying for quite some time.

Most people walk around with a limited belief that

money is some elusive, slippery, magical force that either blesses you or ignores you entirely. Like money is some sexy ex who only comes around when you are not texting first.

This is why folks say things like, "Money does not grow on trees," or "If I just get lucky," or my personal favorite, "Some people just got it like that." It is as if abundance was handed out on the first day of school, but you missed it because you were crying over your crush in the bathroom. But you did not miss it. You just were not taught to see it differently.

Money is not outside of you. It is an extension of your consciousness, mirroring back your beliefs, frequency, and relationship with worthiness. If you believe money is hard to get, it will prove you right. If you believe money flows easily and consistently to you, it will also prove you right. Money is loyal to your inner world. It flows to the version of you that knows how to hold it, respect it, and expect it.

That is right. Expect it. Not pine for it. Do not plead with the Universe as if it were customer service. But expect it the same way you expect your next breath.

You do not get what you want; you get what you are. You cannot manifest money by wishing for it because it is not a genie in a lamp. You manifest money by aligning with the version of yourself who already has it. That version of you does not flinch when checking their bank account or ask, "Can I afford it?" before ordering guac. That version of you knows that abundance is not a reward; it is a natural state of being.

There is the "If I have more, others have less" myth. This is a poverty mindset wrapped in moral guilt.

Although it sounds noble, it is really just another excuse. You say things like, "I do not need that much money; I just want to be comfortable," "I would feel bad having a lot when others are struggling," or "Rich people are greedy."

Being broke does not help poor people. Being abundant allows you to give, build, invest, and uplift others from a place of overflow. Imagine showing up to a potluck with no dish because you did not want to bring "too much." That is what you are doing with money. You cannot feed others from an empty table.

What about the "I have to work hard for money" program? You have been conditioned to believe that unless you are tired, stressed, and sacrificing your joy, you have not earned the money. Rest? That is lazy. Ease? That is suspicious. Flow? It must be a scam. Effort and value are not the same thing. Just because something is hard does not mean it is more valuable. You do not get extra credit in the Universe for burning out.

Let's take two people: one works eighty hours a week as a warehouse worker, hustling overtime just to bring in $60,000 a year. The other is a content creator working ten focused hours a week and making $120,000 with digital products. Who do we glorify? The one breaking their back. Why? Because we have been conditioned to idolize struggle and call it character. We applaud the exhaustion and say, "They are a hard worker," as if it were a badge of honor, even when it is killing them.

And the "That is for people like them" block. This one sounds like: "People like me do not live like that," "I did not grow up with money," "We do not do that in my family." Money has no clue what zip code you were born in. It does not care if you grew up on food stamps or filet mignon. Money is not checking for your past; it is responding to your present frequency. And if you keep telling yourself that wealth is for "other" people, guess what? You will always be "not them." You will stay in your financial friend zone, never daring to make a move on the wealth that is rightfully yours.

Have you ever watched someone go to a restaurant and suddenly develop a PhD in menu prices? They will be like, "Okay, if I order the side salad, no drink, and I tip 13.5%, I will still have $11.17 left in my bank account. That is enough for gas if I drive with the windows down and only take right turns."

Why do we do this? Because deep down, we do not believe we are allowed to have nice things unless we "deserve" them, and we certainly do not believe we can receive anything without proving our worth. Stop asking for permission to want more or have more. Wanting is enough.

Many belief systems about money are rooted in myth. Take the "One Day When" delusion. This is when you say things like, "One day when I make more money, I will be able to do X, Y, Z." That's cute, but "One Day When" is not a calendar date. It is a delay tactic created by fear and limitation, disguised as a comfortable excuse. Because if "One Day" never comes, you never have to change. You never have to challenge your beliefs. You never have to glow up.

Then there is the "Discount Syndrome" delusion that has some of you wrapped around catching sales. I am not talking about being smart with your money or whether something is worthy of its full price. Have you ever seen something beautiful and said, "I love it, but not for that price"? That sentence is just a reflection of your relationship with worth. You do not believe you are worth that price. So you try to shrink abundance to match your mindset instead of expanding your mindset to match your abundance. See the trap?

People glorify struggle, and you hear folks say things like, "I work so hard, I never take a vacation," as if it's honorable. No. It's a sign that you need to rest. Abundance is not about grinding yourself into the ground; it is about being supported so you can thrive.

You do not have to earn your rest. You do not have to suffer to deserve soft moments. You do not have to be in pain to be worthy of abundance. That is not divine. That is generational trauma.

When people say they "do not have money," they usually mean that they do not feel safe receiving money, that they do not believe they deserve that much money, or that they are afraid of what people will think if they suddenly have more money than they do.

These are not surface-level issues. They are deep-rooted, limiting beliefs that manifest into real experiences. You block money when your mind is trained to push it away. You ghost money and then wonder why it does not call you back.

Money is a symbol, mirror, and magnifier of the power you already have—or the lack of belief you have in it. If you think having money makes you better, you will always chase it from a place of insecurity. And if you think money is "bad," "evil," or "corrupts people," guess what you will never allow yourself to become?

You cannot manifest what you secretly judge, and the Universe will not drop a Chanel bag into the lap of someone who energetically side-eyes the person who already has it.

Many people are surprised to hear that they have already experienced money coming to them easily. They just did not realize it because no one is taught to spot it. Have you ever found cash in an old coat pocket? That random $20 that made your whole day? Have you ever had a friend cover your meal and say, "I got you," when you did not even ask? What about the refund you were not expecting? The deposit that hit early? That was not luck. That was money flowing easily to you without you having to force it.

Remember when you sold something online and it was gone within minutes? Or when someone sent you a tip just because they appreciated your work? Or when your parent, partner, or friend slid you a little extra "just in case"? You were not grinding or hustling. You were not manifesting under a full moon with six crystals and a raven feather. Money simply arrived because you were open enough to receive it.

Think about every time you got a raise without begging for it. Every bonus you did not expect. Every birthday card with a little cash tucked inside. Did you chase? No. Did you struggle? No. You just allowed it to flow to you.

Have you ever received a complimentary coffee? Gotten a discount without asking? Had someone randomly pay for your gas? Found a gift card in your drawer that you forgot you had? That is the Universe saying, "Look how easy this can be when you stop gripping so tight."

Remember when you walked into T.J. Maxx for one thing, and they happened to have it on sale? Or when you returned something and they gave you more back than you paid? *That is what abundance looks like.*

The Venmo payment you forgot someone owed you. The client who showed up without you promoting anything. The babysitting gig, the side hustle, the affiliate link, the cashback reward, the refund from a canceled flight. All of it is money. All of it came with ease. And it came because, for a moment, you were not resisting. You were just… open.

We are conditioned to dismiss those moments by calling them flukes or coincidences. But the more you acknowledge them, the more they compound. When you treat every little win like proof that money loves you, you invite more. When you say, "See? That was easy," you create momentum.

Think about how many times money arrived without you trying to control it. Now imagine what would happen if you expected that all the time. Welcomed it. Built your next-level identity around it. If it happened once, it can happen again. And if it has happened dozens of times, then it is already a pattern; you just didn't notice it.

Let go of the belief that you have to "deserve" it because money came to you when you were doing nothing. Money has never been the problem; your limited belief was. The proof is in your life.

Struggle is not a noble act; it is a learned mindset that can, thankfully, be unlearned. You were not put on this Earth to suffer your way to heaven, and you certainly were not sent here to earn your worth through hardship or to prove yourself through pain. Somewhere along the line, we got handed this blueprint for life that said, "If you want good things, you have to bleed for them first." Most people took it, framed it, and built their whole life around it. But this is where we challenge (the second Mystic Key) and reframe it (the third Mystic Key). Struggle is not your destiny; it is a decision.

If you grew up watching people work three jobs while constantly worrying about bills or scraping by, yet still not getting ahead, it's easy to normalize struggle as a rite of passage. You might even find comfort in it because it is familiar. You might even feel guilty when things start going well in your life because you have been trained to expect the other shoe to drop. But just because something is familiar does not mean it is true.

Struggle is the mindset that says you have to pay dues in suffering before you are allowed to live peacefully. It says, "Who do you think you are to have it easy?" "Do not forget where you came from," or "Do not get too comfortable; it could all go away." However, that is not wisdom speaking; it is a manifestation of generational trauma.

You can spot the struggle mindset in statements like: "If I do not do it myself, it will not get done," or "I am used to fighting for everything I have." Sound familiar?

That is not your personality talking. That is a limited belief system stuck in a loop.

Walking away from struggle can feel uncomfortable at first because if you have always had to fight, then peace might feel like laziness or cheating. To shift from a struggle mindset to a money mindset, you must first become aware of what you have normalized. A struggle mindset is built on assumptions, and it assumes that unless something is difficult, it is not valuable. You end up training yourself to brace for impact, lower your expectations, and keep your dreams modest so you do not get hurt.

To transform it, you must reject those assumptions outright. We do not negotiate with terrorists. You are the captain of the bomb squad dismantling the limited belief (the second Mystic Key).

The first shift is recognizing that your current financial reality is not permanent. People like to declare that it's a life sentence, but it's not that either. It is a reflection of past thoughts, past beliefs, and past energy. Once you understand that, you realize your money story is not a fixed one; it is fluid. Money responds to your dominant frequency, meaning you do not have to "earn" your way into a better life. You simply shift into it by embodying new, more expansive beliefs.

A money mindset is not about how much you currently have; it is about how you relate to what you have and what you believe is possible for you. Where the struggle mindset says, "This is all there is," the money mindset says, "This is the beginning." It means stopping yourself mid-thought when your mind thinks,

"That is too expensive," and replacing it with, "That is expansive, and I am moving into it."

It means noticing when you flinch at nice things and reminding yourself that you are worthy of nice things, even if no one ever taught you how to receive them.

The money mindset requires a new standard of identity, your next-level self. You cannot hold onto the old version of yourself, the one who expects bills to be tight and feels guilt around spending, and step into abundance at the same time. You must release your outdated self-image and shed the version of you who made struggle part of your identity.

That means making choices from faith, not fear, and spending like someone who trusts money will return. It means charging your worth, saying no to misaligned opportunities, and expecting to be compensated with respect and overflow. You must expect it.

This transformation is not about pretending to be rich. It's about recognizing that your thoughts are a magnet for abundance, and your mindset is your currency.

———

Now that you understand how the struggle mindset operates, let's discuss what you can do to shift into a money mindset that manifests overflow.

audit your money beliefs

Grab a journal and write down everything you believe about money. And I mean everything. Especially the things you have been afraid to admit out loud. Start with:

1. "Money is…"
2. "People with money are…"
3. "I cannot have more money because…"

Write it without censorship and then circle back and ask, "Is this actually true?" "Who taught me this?" "What does this belief create in my life?" If it is not aligned with abundance, it goes.

upgrade your money language

Words are spells, and every time you say, "I am broke," you reinforce lack and broke-ness. Every time you say, "I cannot afford that," you reinforce struggle as part of your energy field. Instead, start using empowered language.

1. Replace "I am broke" with "I am in a temporary cash-flow pause."
2. Replace "I cannot afford it" with "How can I create that?"
3. Replace "I do not know where the money is coming from" with "Money always finds its way to me."

Your Universe listens when you speak, so it would be wise to stop telling it lies. Speak as the next-level version of you who knows the bag is already theirs.

acknowledge your money

If you spend your energy avoiding looking at your bank account, then you are treating money like a threat. Stop ghosting your finances. Instead, acknowledge every dollar that comes in, no matter how small, and express your gratitude. Found a quarter on the street? Thank you. Got a $2 Venmo payment from a friend? Thank you. Gratitude is the frequency of expansion. The more you acknowledge and appreciate your money, the more it multiplies.

spend from a place of power, not panic

Before you swipe your card, pause for a moment. Ask yourself, "Am I spending from a place of power or panic?" Spending from panic sounds like: "I better get this now before I cannot afford it later." Spending from a place of power sounds like: "This supports my next-level self, and I trust more is coming." When you make purchases from a place of power, not panic, you circulate abundance, not scarcity.

release guilt around receiving

Practice receiving compliments, gifts, support, and unexpected income without guilt. Receiving with ease is a skill that requires development. Many people block money not because they cannot make it, but because they do not feel worthy of having it. Desiring more is not a burden to yourself, your family, or society. You are not greedy for wanting luxury, and you are not shallow for dreaming bigger. Money is not the problem; your shame is. Let it go.

affirm daily: "i don't struggle anymore."

Say it. Out loud. Every day.

Write it on sticky notes that you post on your bathroom mirror. Set it as your phone wallpaper so you're reminded every time you unlock your screen. Tattoo it on your soul if you have to. The more you affirm it, the more you live it. And the more you live it, the more your external reality begins to align with the new frequency you have claimed for your life.

You didn't wake up to do the inner work, face your shadows, rewire your beliefs, and rewrite your entire story just to struggle with money. That is not your path anymore.

The real glow-up is not just about self-worth; it is also about stepping into total, unapologetic receivership and allowing life to reward you. Not because you have hustled hard enough to finally be worthy, but because you have remembered the truth, which is that you have *always* been worthy.

---

glow-up activation: brokie behavior

Write down all the brokie behaviors you have been engaging in that actively keep you poor or stuck in scarcity. Call yourself out. Is it that you only buy cheap stuff because you are too scared to invest in yourself? Maybe you do not ask for what you are worth because, deep down, you think you do not deserve it. How about you keep playing small and avoiding opportunities because you are terrified of failure (or success, let's be real)? Is it that you think living paycheck to paycheck is "enough," and that real wealth is for other people, not you?

Now that you have confronted your brokie behaviors, you are going to do something that screams abundance. Do something that completely flips your brokie patterns and forces you to step into your new identity as someone who attracts wealth and abundance. Enroll in that course, book that trip you've been putting off, get a new wardrobe, raise your rates or prices, apply for the role, or commit to buying the software you need for your business. With this, you are saying, "I am worthy of the wealth I am attracting."

rewrite the rules

Redefine Success on Your Own Terms

YOUR SUCCESS IS up to you, and only you are qualified to decide which endeavors you will count toward your success. The opinions of other people have no weight here. It is easy to get caught up in the game of life, and when you do, it can have you believing that your 7th-grade teacher's critical opinion of your essay was actually true. But what if it wasn't? What if that person were someone who lost the ability to see the beauty of the world through the lens of a 7th grader? And what if their inability to see made their assessment of your work wrong because they were looking through the wrong lens?

You see, most people lack vision. Not because they are inherently incapable of seeing, but because society has stripped them of their ability to imagine and dream. Because of this, opinions of your work are often flawed and clouded in self-judgment that has been projected onto you by the person judging your work. You have then taken these assessments, covered under the illusion of authority because maybe they came from a teacher, a parent, a mentor, or a boss, and you have accepted them as a universal truth in your life.

You are in the process of rewiring your belief systems and rewriting your story. Part of that means rewriting the rules of the game you have been playing so that you win the game every time. And because you have new rules, you are redefining what success looks like for you. Is this cheating? Not if you write it into the rules.

Your idea of success must change because the rules of your old success came from an outdated game that you are no longer playing. It is like still trying to win points in dodgeball when the new game is chess. You are over here ducking and diving, trying not to get hit by rubber balls, while everyone else has moved to the table, calmly moving knights and pawns. Of course, it no longer makes sense. Of course, it feels like you are losing. You're not even playing the right game.

But a golden secret no one tells you is that you get to change the game entirely. You get to choose the arena, define the objective, and decide when you have won.

Let that sink in for a moment.

You have been living under rules you did not create, standards you did not choose, and definitions of success that were handed down to you by people who never even knew you. People who were not equipped to see the fullness of your vision. People who lacked the imagination, capacity, or permission to define their own success, so instead, they downloaded someone else's version of success and passed it along like a virus. And here you are, still living by it.

You're not here to be good at someone else's game.

You are not here to live up to someone else's metric of achievement, not when those metrics were never designed to hold the vastness of who you are. The world loves a clean little box to place people in. And when you do not fit, it calls you lost, lazy, weird, rebellious, unrealistic, too much, too loud, too sensitive, too ambitious, not enough. But what if none of that is actually true?

What if you are just someone who was never meant to fit inside the box to begin with? What if success for you looks like being free? Free to move, free to rest, free to create without having to monetize every moment or turn your hobbies into hustles. What if success looks like peace? Like living in a home that holds you, drinking your tea slowly in the morning, writing when the inspiration strikes, and walking away when it does not. What if success looks like not proving anything to anyone ever again?

See, here is what they get wrong. The world tells you that success is loud. That it is measurable and has a dollar amount, a square footage, a title, or a ranking. Or that it comes with a blue check, a plaque, a party, or a press release. And I am not saying those things are not beautiful or worth celebrating. I am saying they are not the only indicators of a life well-lived. Because some of the most successful people I know have none of those things, and some of the most miserable people I have met have all of them.

We were told that success was linear. Do this, then this, then that, and then you are allowed to be proud of yourself. Then you can rest and retire when your body is too old for international travel. Then you have made it. However, what they did not tell us is that the goalposts move, and the system keeps redefining the criteria, so you never actually feel like you have arrived.

You get the degree, and then they ask for experience. You get the experience, and then they ask for another degree. You get the job, and then suddenly, it is about getting the promotion. You get the promotion, and now it is about how fast you can climb the career ladder, how well you can perform even at the expense of your health, and how much more you can produce. It never ends. You are always running, chasing, reaching, trying to "become" something that someone else decided was worth becoming. You have been running from this invisible force that is constantly breathing down the back of your neck.

But what if you are already successful exactly as you are at this moment? What if the only thing that is missing is your decision to own your success and claim it as yours, in spite of the game you were taught to play?

You get to choose the moment you become successful. Maybe it was the first time you said no to something that did not feel right, or maybe it was the day you honored your mental health over your deadlines. Maybe it was when you walked away from a relationship, a job, or a pattern that was breaking you down. Maybe it is right now, this exact moment, when you finally realize you no longer need anyone's permission to define yourself.

Your definition of success must be deeply personal, so personal that no one else fully understands it. The definition you create must be made exclusively for you and custom-tailored to your soul's blueprint. It has to resonate in your chest, not on your LinkedIn profile. It has to feel like alignment, not achievement. You are not a resume. You are a living, breathing, divine being on your own timeline. And that alone is enough.

In addition to reclaiming your own story, you must refuse to allow systems built on exploitation, racism, patriarchy, capitalism, and outdated structures to tell you whether you are worthy or not.

You do not need more credentials. You need to know, deep in your bones, that your work is worthy because you are. That your path is valid because you chose it. That your glow-up is real because you said so.

Rewriting the rules does not just give you more power; it gives you freedom. Real, deep, soul-level freedom. The kind that makes you exhale in your chest and think, "Ohhh... so this is what peace feels like."

Most of us do not realize we have even been playing by rules, let alone outdated ones, until one day, we look around and think, "Wait... why am I doing this? Who said this was required?" That is when you start to crack the code. That is when your freedom starts to peek its head out like, "Remember me?"

And the best part is that you have already rewritten the rules in your life many times. You just didn't call it that at the time or recognize that it was what you were doing.

You know that moment when you stopped texting back out of obligation? When you used to respond to every "wyd," like it was your civic duty, but then one day you were like, "Actually... I am not doing this anymore." That was you rewriting the rule that says you owe people constant access to your time and energy.

Or the first time you took a nap in the middle of the day, without guilt, without trying to "earn it" by finishing everything on your to-do list. That was you breaking the rule that rest must be a reward instead of a right.

Maybe it was when you stopped forcing yourself to finish books you were not enjoying just because someone on TikTok said it was a "must-read." You quietly closed the book, slid it back on the shelf, and gave yourself full permission not to finish it with any shame. That right there? Liberation.

We have all had these moments of tiny rebellions that may not seem significant on the outside, but on the inside, they are spiritual revolutions. You thought you were just skipping the birthday party you didn't want to attend because Pam was never all that nice to you anyway. But really? You were reclaiming your time and honoring your energy by declaring that you are not a social obligation to be fulfilled.

Every time you say no to something that no longer aligns with you, you are rewriting a rule. And every time you say yes to something that brings you joy, even if no one else understands it, you are rewriting a rule.

Some of the rules we were following were truly ridiculous anyway. Like, "Do not wear white after Labor Day." What in the colonial nonsense is that? Or the one that says you cannot have breakfast for dinner. Please. I have had waffles at 10 p.m. and felt closer to God than I ever have in a morning meeting.

However, some of the more harmful rules are

sneakier. They dress themselves up as "standards" or "norms." They tell you things like, "You cannot be taken seriously if you change your mind," "You cannot quit a job without having another one lined up," "You should not speak up unless you are 100% sure you are right," and "You have to prove you are struggling in order to deserve a break." Rule after rule after capitalistic rule. I think I speak for everyone when I say to society, "Just shut up!"

These rules are quiet, but they are loud in your body. You feel them when you hesitate to ask for help, when you shrink yourself in rooms where you should be standing tall, and when you feel guilty for choosing joy over productivity.

So much of personal freedom is about catching those quiet rules, those subconscious contracts you signed years ago without realizing it, and then deciding you are no longer available for them.

When you rewrite a rule, you stop being a character in someone else's story and start being the narrator of your own. You stop being someone who reacts to life and start becoming someone who designs it.

Let us also discuss how rewriting the rules does not always feel glamorous in the moment. You may not initially feel big and strong, and sometimes it feels awkward, as if you are doing something wrong. Like the first time you leave a toxic job without a new one lined up. You tell your friends you are "in transition" or "in between jobs," which is code for "I am figuring it out and trying not to panic." But every part of your spirit knows you had to go and that staying would have been the real betrayal.

Or the first time you tell your family, "Actually, I do not want kids," or "I am not going to church anymore," or "I do not care about being married." Whew. The tension that fills the room could be sliced with a dull knife. You can practically hear the generational programming glitching in the background. But guess what? That is you breaking free from inherited expectations, and that is sacred work.

The freedom does not always come instantly. Sometimes, it arrives in the quiet that follows, such as the first peaceful morning, or the slow return of your energy. The way your spirit starts to feel is that it is no longer suffocating inside the shell of who you used to be.

―――――

You have realized that the old rules no longer apply. Good. Now let's talk about how to break them on purpose, because when you rewrite the rules, you redefine success and start living by your own definition.

identify the unspoken rule

You cannot redefine success if you are still trying to win at someone else's game. Most of us follow silent rules, such as "You are only successful if you are productive," "You are only worthy if you are performing," and "You are only valuable if other people approve of you."

Success, by those definitions, is exhausting and never enough. These standards are impossible to satisfy because the goalpost always moves. But once you realize you have been playing by invisible rules you did not create, you can ask yourself, "Do I even agree with this?" That is the start of your newfound freedom.

name the source of the rule

Was it your mom? Your high school coach? Society? Capitalism?

Once you name the source of the rule, it stops feeling like a universal truth and starts looking like what it really is: someone else's projection. You stop measuring your life by the standards of people who do not even live the life you want and have never lived the life they wanted. You reclaim the authority to decide what achievement looks like for you. That is success.

define the new rule in your own words

If the old rule was: "I have to grind to prove I deserve abundance," your new rule might be: "My joy and peace are my most valuable currency." That new rule becomes your new definition of success. No more success being measured by hustle, struggle, or burnout. Now, it is measured by alignment, freedom, and how lit up you feel inside.

break the old rule

You do not fully embody a new definition of success by writing it on a sticky note. You must *live* it.

You walk away from what drains you, and you say no when other people expect you to say yes. Allow your life to start reflecting your truth. Every time you act differently and move like it, you are teaching your body that this is what success looks like now.

set boundaries

Success used to mean being liked because you were nice and accommodating. Now? Your success might mean being misunderstood because you are finally being honest.

Setting boundaries is how you protect your new rules, and every time you do so, you will affirm: "My time, energy, and peace are the metrics now." Not approval, compliance, or burnout.

let people be confused

People might be confused, disappointed, or even offended by your new rules, as if you have personally attacked them for choosing your freedom. But part of redefining success means you no longer live for their understanding. You are no longer chasing external validation because you are building a life that feels right to you. When you are free from the need to be understood, that is success.

celebrate yourself

Your old success needed a trophy or a raise to feel validated, but your new success celebrates the everyday glow-ups. You honored your energy. A win. You did not over-explain yourself. A win. You put yourself first. A win. When you celebrate these micro-shifts, you teach your system that these moments matter and that *this* is what your success looks like now.

notice who you become without the rule

When the old rules start to fall away, you finally get to meet the real you. Perhaps it's the first time you've ever seen yourself. But this is the version of you that owes nothing to anyone.

Success becomes less about what you *achieve* and more about who you *get to be*. Are you softer than you were when you were pretending to be something you're not? Are you more honest than you were when you only said things you thought people wanted to hear? Are you more present with your children now that you have identified that work does not, in fact, come first? That is the new success.

give yourself permission

Redefining success means you no longer need external permission to feel worthy, deserving, or proud of yourself. You give it to yourself, and you get to have it right now. You say: "This version of me is already enough. I am already successful because I said so." Real success is not a finish line; it is a feeling, a way of being, and a decision. You reach your next level just by choosing yourself.

Rewriting the rules and redefining success creates space for the real you to emerge. You don't need to pretend to be something you're not, prove, or explain yourself. You begin to show up in alignment with your soul and not your resume. You become the one who is no longer living according to the borrowed dreams of those who neglected to try or the expired standards from a time that probably should have never existed.

Even though it might not always be easy, it will always be worth it. Because when you rewrite the rules, you stop chasing the life that was never meant for you and start creating the one that is. You stop living as if you're on borrowed time and start living as if the clock were always yours to set. You stop waiting for permission and start moving with your own conviction.

And the beautiful irony is that when you do that, life will go out of its way to meet you there. Opportunities will shift because, suddenly, you are now available to accept them. You become lighter, freer, and more you.

And the people who were meant to see you, the real you, can finally recognize you because you have stepped out from behind the mask that prevented you from being who you were supposed to be, and told you success only looked one way.

But now? That is done. Because the silent agreement for rewriting the rules is that your life will inevitably change, and isn't that what we incarnated here for?

———

glow-up activation: the glow-up manifesto

Write a manifesto declaring what success means to you on your terms. Use this manifesto to break down the norms of society and redefine success according to your own vision. Be bold and fearless in your declarations. Your declarations should scare you. This is your permission to live authentically and fully.

the coronation

YOU HAVE NOW RECEIVED the 7 Mystic Keys. With these tools, you have everything you need to completely disrupt the narrative that your lineage and society have given you, and write something that not only benefits you but also elevates you into the position you were always meant to hold.

Up until this point, you have been living your life on the free trial version. You got a taste of what you were capable of, but were never able to accept the full, paid version. At times, you caught glimpses of your light and power, but never allowed yourself to experience its expression fully. You only experienced your brilliance in moderation, and this made it difficult for you to move through the world as the person you were always meant to be, causing you to wither away, and occasionally forget who you were, slowly.

Accept this book as your coronation, because by using the keys, you are crowning your soul and accepting yourself as a sovereign being. And as a new sovereign being, let me give you your first briefing and set of instructions for sitting on your newfound throne.

Newly crowned royalty should always move with their manifesto in mind. Your manifesto is your declaration of truth and your sacred rebellion against imposed limitations, whether it is self-imposed or thrust upon you. Your manifesto is your personal decree and a call to action for your soul.

It is time for you to deliver a new set of instructions to reality that dictate how reality must organize itself around you. You are now sovereign, and therefore, it is up to you to decide how you interact with the world and how the world is now permitted to interact with you. What happened in the past is now gone, but what will happen in the future is subject to your control, and reality is your subject. The past may have taught you, but it no longer defines who you are.

Your manifesto is your law, and you are the highest governing authority. No one can change the laws in your manifesto except for you. Remember to administer your new boundaries and enforce your manifesto when those boundaries are violated.

You started this process doubting who you were and what you were capable of. You questioned how much you had to give to be enough and what you had to do to be accepted by the ones you loved. You beat yourself up for human mistakes, and forgot to show yourself compassion for simply having learning experiences that taught you about the world. You would try something new, only to be met with less-than-favorable results, and then swear never to try it again. You convince yourself that you were a failure because you caught someone smirking when you missed the mark; however, that time of self-deprecation has come to an end.

Today is the day you step into your next-level version, and in this version, your expectations have elevated. Today, you stop taking "no" for an answer and start saying "yes" to yourself. You don't ask for permission. You don't ask for approval. You don't hand over your power to someone who has yet to claim their own.

It is time for you to remember that in all lifetimes, and in all realities, you were always worthy. You were always special. You were always loved. You were always smart. You were always funny. You were always creative. You were always beautiful. You were always learning. You were always growing. You were always healing. You were always deserving. It was always your turn. You never had to wait.

You were always enough.

The glow-up is complete.

afterword

If you have made it to the end, it is important to know that you are not the same person you were when you began reading this book. Something has shifted in you, and in time it will come to the surface. A part of you has awakened, and that voice inside, which has always known you were meant for more, has started to speak a little louder.

This was not just a book. It was a key. Now that you have received it, it's time to use it to unlock the doors of opportunity for yourself.

Glow-ups are not just surface-level transformations. They are spiritual awakenings in disguise, meant to awaken the part of you that has been sleeping. They are the moment your soul stands up and says, *"I am ready to be me."*

Revisit these pages when you forget your power and speak these truths out loud when the world tries to make you doubt yourself. Most of all, keep glowing because your light is not a phase; it is your birthright.

The end. And the beginning.

mystic rainn
The Mystic Maven

Mystic Rainn, also known as The Mystic Maven, is an author, spiritual visionary, mindset coach, and transformative voice in the world of modern mysticism. She helps others reconnect with their inner wisdom, trust their intuition, and awaken the divine power within.

Known for her bold presence and soul-shifting messages, Mystic Rainn creates spaces where spiritual seekers become sovereign leaders in their own lives. Her teachings blend timeless metaphysical truths with grounded, actionable guidance, inviting seekers not just to heal but to rise, glow, and fully embody their higher, next-level selves.

When you engage with Mystic Rainn's work, expect transformation, truth, and an empowering return to who you truly are.

- amazon.com/author/mysticrainn
- facebook.com/iammysticrainn
- instagram.com/iammysticrainn
- youtube.com/@MysticRainn

also by mystic rainn

The Glow-Up Manifesto Journal: 103 Unapologetic Daily Prompts to Activate Your Glow-Up

The Fool's Guide to Tarot: A No-Nonsense Guide to Tarot Reading and Understanding Tarot Card Meanings

www.ingramcontent.com/pod-product-compliance
Lightning Source LLC
Chambersburg PA
CBHW050525100526
44581CB00008B/138/J